TRAVELLERS

EAST COAST
AUSTRALIA

By
DAR

Written by Darroch Donald
Original photography by Rebecca Robinson

Published by Thomas Cook Publishing
A division of Thomas Cook Tour Operations Limited.
Company registration no. 1450464 England
The Thomas Cook Business Park, Unit 9, Coningsby Road,
Peterborough PE3 8SB, United Kingdom
E-mail: books@thomascook.com, Tel: + 44 (0) 1733 416477
www.thomascookpublishing.com

Produced by Cambridge Publishing Management Limited
Burr Elm Court, Main Street, Caldecote CB23 7NU

ISBN: 978-1-84157-818-7

First edition © 2008 Thomas Cook Pu
Text © Thomas Cook Publishing
Maps © Thomas Cook Publishing/PC

Series Editor: Maisie Fitzpatrick
Production/DTP: Steven Collins

Printed and bound in Italy by Printer

Cover photography: Front L–R: © Aus
© Gerald Nowak/Alamy; © World Pict
Back L–R: © Neil Farrin/Jon Arnold In
© Shaun Cunningham/Alamy

The paper used for this book has been independently certified as having
been sourced from well-managed forests and recycled wood or fibre
according to the rules of the Forest Stewardship Council.
This book has been printed and bound in Italy by Printer Trento S.r.l.,
an FSC certified company for printing books on FSC mixed paper in
compliance with the chain of custody and on products labelling standards.

FSC

Mixed Sources
Product group from well-managed
forests and recycled wood or fibre

Cert no. CQ-COC-000012
www.fsc.org
© 1996 Forest Stewardship Council

Contents

Introduction

Planning a trip 'Down Under' is a bit like being given an empty supermarket trolley for a three-minute 'dash and grab': you realise time is of the essence but feel overwhelmed with both opportunity and choice. First, there is the Sydney department – the 'must see' Opera House and Bondi Beach. Then, the activity section: will a surfboard fit in the trolley? And the Gold Coast or the Great Barrier Reef – can you hug a koala quickly somewhere between the king prawns and the didgeridoos? Well, don't panic. Even with a trolley only half full, you'll have one mighty shop.

Blessed with some of the most recognisable icons and beautiful landscapes in the world, rich in natural assets, huge in both size and character and living up to all expectations, Australia is one country you simply have to get to know, and the East Coast is the perfect place to start.

At over 7.5 million sq km (almost 3 million sq miles), the great island continent (as it is often referred to) is about the same size as the USA and about 32 times the size of the UK. In Australia size matters. Skies are not just big here, they are oceanic. The country can alter your entire concept of space, often starting with the time and effort it takes to arrive. To fully explore it would take a lifetime and, indeed, a few try. But for most of us, sadly, time is short and we rightly choose a hectic tour of the East Coast as the ideal precursor. But if you make the effort and the journey, one thing is certain – you will not be disappointed.

When it comes to tourism appeal, Australia has considerable expectations to meet. It is not so much a destination as a brand. Think 'Australia' and instantly the sun is shining, you're on the beach or beside the Opera House,

Surfers catching the waves at Coolangatta, Queensland

The Opera House at dawn, taken near the Botanical Gardens

while the outback also beckons with its kangaroos, koalas and gum trees. But Australia is so much more than that.

With Sydney as an arrival point, you are off to a fine start. At Circular Quay behold the Opera House and Harbour Bridge. Immediately you will see that icons can actually be bigger than the imagination, and the great southern city really is one of the most beautiful on earth. But Sydney is only the beginning – the country's modern, human and urban façade. Manage to extricate yourself from her spell and the door is opened on that other Australia, its magical and ancient natural environment and its unique wildlife. With almost as many national parks as beaches, natural Australia is very much part of the holiday experience and whether it is the laugh of the kookaburra or the smell of eucalyptus suffusing the night air, such memories will never leave you.

The East Coast also offers endless opportunities to try new activities, from four-wheel driving on Fraser Island to scuba-diving on the Great Barrier Reef, and all of it within 'cooee' of that seemingly omnipresent beach and the sound of surf as your constant travel companion.

So, welcome to the 'Lucky Country', a place where simple journeys can become epics, and mere holidays odysseys. It's time to fall in love with Australia, make her acquaintance and forever keep in touch.

Oh, and you had better bring a diary – a big one.

Legend:
- City
- Large Town
- Small Town
- POI
- Main Road
- Minor Road
- Airport
- Railway

Coral Sea

GREAT BARRIER REEF

Mackay

Oxford Downs

Collinsville

Mount Dalrymple
1277

Townsville

Billabong Wildlife Sanctuary

A1

Moranbah

Mount Coolon

Orpheus Island

Hinchinbrook Island

Tully

Fitzroy Island

CAIRNS

Bartle Frere
1612

Cairns International

Pentland

Greenvale

Undara Volcanic NP

Lizard Island

Hope Vale

Cape Tribulation

Cooktown

Daintree

Mossman

Chillagoe

GREAT DIVIDING RANGE

Corfield

Richmond

Stamford

Winton

A2

Townsville International

Lockhart River

Coen

Cape York Peninsula

Kowanyama

Pormpuraaw

Weipa

Croydon

Stamford

QUEENSLAND

A1

Cloncurry

83

Wellesley Islands

Karumba

Gregory Downs

Gulf of Carpentaria

N

Tasman Sea

200km
100 miles
0

BRISBANE
Gold Coast
Murwillumbah
Byron Bay
Coffs Harbour
Bellingen
South West Rocks
Port Macquarie
Forster
Newcastle
The Entrance
SYDNEY
Katoomba
Penrith
Kingsford Smith
Gloucester
Mount Barrington 1585
Armidale
Dorrigo
Grafton
Canungra
Tewantin
Tin Can Bay
Fraser Island
Gympie
Brisbane International
Maryborough
Rockhampton
Heron Island
Lady Musgrave Island
Gladstone
Toowoomba
Emerald
Springsure
Taroom
Roma
Caldervale
Charleville
Cunnamulla
Ta.room
Barcaldine
Longreach
Stonehenge
Windorah
Eromanga
Thargomindah
Grey Range
Hungerford
Goodooga
Bourke
Louth
Walgett
Hermidale
Merrygoen
Darling
Condobolin
Griffith
White Cliffs
Broken Hill
Darnick
Tibooburra
Milparinka
Brighton Downs
Boulia
Bedourie
Innamincka
Sturt Stony Desert
Lyndhurst
Flinders Ranges
Yunta
Peterborough
SOUTH AUSTRALIA
NEW SOUTH WALES
GREAT DIVIDING RANGE

A1
A3
A5
A2
A71
A4
39
49
55
32
34
75
879
A32
39

The land

At over 7.5 million sq km (almost 3 million sq miles), Australia accounts for 5 per cent of the world's land area and is its sixth-largest country. There are 21 million people living in Australia (the USA has 300 million) and not surprisingly – being one of the driest places on earth – the vast majority live along the coastal fringes.

The long and the short of it

The coastal fringes of the eastern states of Queensland, New South Wales and Victoria have by far the highest population densities. This is due in no small part to the Great Dividing Range which adds that vital geological equivalent of a raindance. The majority

'Surf's up' on Sydney's North Shore

of people live in Greater Sydney (4.5 million), or Brisbane and the neighbouring Gold Coast (2.2 million).

The Great Dividing Range, formed over 90 million years ago when New Zealand made its break for geological independence, is an extensive yet relatively narrow range that stretches over 4,000km (2,500 miles) from the far north of Queensland to Tasmania. It is also home to the nation's highest peaks, with the highest, Mount Kosciusko (2,228m/7,300ft), one of only a few in southern New South Wales and northeastern Victoria that can make a brief appointment with snow in winter.

In contrast, the highest peak in the tropical far north of Queensland is Bartle Frere, which at 1,622m (5,320ft) receives no snow but does boast Australia's highest annual rainfall of over 7,000mm (275in). In 2000 it was a record-breaking 12,461mm (490in).

Not surprisingly, Australia's two longest rivers, the Murray and Darling,

The 'Three Sisters', Katoomba, Blue Mountains National Park, NSW

are sourced from the Great Dividing Range, yet, these days very depleted, they join and reach the sea along the south coast in South Australia. The vast Murray Darling Basin is often labelled the food bowl of Australia, but now, after the worst drought on record, it has become the hot topic of social and political debate surrounding climate change and agricultural sustainability.

Diversity and climate

Despite the classic perception of an endless expanse of 'outback' baking under oceanic blue skies, the great island nation actually possesses an astonishingly diverse geography and ecology. Again, this is particularly apparent on the East Coast due to the influence of the Great Dividing Range

and climatic changes due to latitude. In Sydney, halfway up the coast of New South Wales, a temperate climate with mild winters allows seasonal change and subsequent habitats that result in a rich abundance of wildlife, even in the city itself. For the human species it offers the perfect climate, with over 300 sunny days a year and temperatures that very rarely drop below freezing. In contrast, Cairns, 2,800km (1,740 miles) to the north, has a classic tropical climate, with warm, dry winters and uncomfortably hot and humid monsoonal summers. Add to that the coastal topography with its lush rainforest and the iconic and unique Great Barrier Reef, and you have one of the richest, most precious biodiversities on the planet.

Climate change in Australia

Given Australia's dry climate, it is miraculous that it has managed to become such a well-developed nation capable of sustaining a population of 21 million people. But the tragedy is that even without the threat of climate change, this simple reality is something to which the vast majority of Australians are oblivious. But maybe, just maybe, with an increasing awareness and in tune with the growing global trend, things are changing.

Hole in the bucket

It was not so long ago (1788) that a hapless, starving mob of colonists

Melbourne supply dam Sugarloaf at 20 per cent capacity, 2007

from the First Fleet stood in abject misery in the middle of their failed veggie garden. No doubt they did so under the gaze of bemused Aboriginals, who, after thousands of years of highly successful sustainable living, and having never seen a prize carrot in their life, must have thought the behaviour almost comical.

But the fact is, in money-driven, predominantly urban-based 'white' Australia, little has really changed. With a population already on the cusp of credible environmental sustainability and global climate change now as sure a reality as the Aboriginals' demise, it seems the lessons learned by the Aborigine so long ago have not been heeded.

Cause and effect

In Australia, like almost everywhere else, the great debate about climate change rages with an increasing intensity. Statistics are bandied about and debated, promoted by some, over-scrutinised or vehemently denied by others.

It is already a well-known fact that Australians have one of the largest emission footprints per capita on the planet. However, it has only recently become generally accepted that the

Rain is rare in the outback, but when it rains, it pours

detrimental effects of climate change are unequivocal, very serious and will become increasingly so.

The key scientific conclusions are that by 2030, temperatures in Australia will rise by about 1°C (2°F) and increase by up to 5°C (10°F) by the end of the century. There will be changes in temperature extremes and decreases in annual average rainfall. Also, when it does rain, rainfall is likely to be more intense. Other findings include: the likelihood of more frequent droughts; increased high fire danger; the probability of tropical cyclones becoming more intense; and the continuing rise of sea levels.

With a nation already in the grip of a dire and lengthy drought, staple crops failing nationwide and the Great Barrier Reef long threatened with total annihilation due to rising ocean temperatures, these predictions – be they credible or not – hardly make for prize carrots.

However, at last it seems the words 'climate' and 'change' have become fashionable. Driven by media hype, it has suddenly become trendy and practical to have solar panels on the roof, or to switch off redundant lights, walk, or cycle to work. It is not alternative to be 'Green' anymore, but cool and responsible. Caring for the environment can even be financially profitable – it can actually save you money.

Hopefully the hype will last, but one thing is for sure in Australia: climate change is beginning to hurt and hurt badly, and the nation now offers a fine example of a very innate human behaviour – that only when hurt, or directed *ad populum*, so to speak, will most people act.

History

60,000–40,000 BC onwards Long before European settlers arrive and for many thousands of years, Aboriginals live a sustainable existence in harmony with the environment.

AD 1770 On his great voyage of discovery, James Cook makes landfall, naming the location Botany Bay. Continuing north, he suffers a disastrous encounter with the Great Barrier Reef, running aground near what was aptly named Cape Tribulation. Forced to stop for two months to make repairs, he establishes Cooktown.

1786 To ease a burgeoning prison population, King George III of England decides the 'new lands' would make a fine penal colony.

1788 The 'First Fleet', comprising six vessels carrying about 300 crew and 800 convicts, sails in to Botany Bay under the command of Captain Arthur Phillip. After an amicable encounter with Aboriginals, Phillip finds suitable anchorage and names Sydney Cove after the British secretary of state Viscount Sydney. Phillip himself is sworn in as first governor of the newly proclaimed state of New South Wales.

1779–90 Attempts at settlement prove disastrous. The crew is poorly supplied and unskilled in utilising local resources. The local Eora Aboriginals fall victim to the settlers' superior attitude and the new diseases they introduce. Numbers decrease rapidly. Then more favourable soils for crops are discovered further up the harbour at Parramatta.

1790–1810 Sydney develops with the arrival of more convicts and the parole of others. Phillip departs, leaving soldiers in charge of the convicts. They grant each other rights to secure tracts of land and use convict labour to work on them. In the absence of money, rum becomes the currency of choice. Chaos ensues. England's first attempt to restore order in the person of Captain Bligh (of *Mutiny on the Bounty* fame) fails. New governor Scot Lachlan Macquarie finally succeeds.

1823   Surveyor-general John Oxley is dispatched north to establish a new penal colony. He does so on the banks of the newly named Brisbane River, in effect creating the settlement of the same name.

1840–42   The transportation of convicts to New South Wales is abolished. The penal colony in Brisbane is also officially closed and Queensland follows NSW in opening up to free settlement.

1850   New farms and settlements are established apace. Wool and wheat production in particular forms a solid base economy. Explorers Lawson, Blaxland and Wentworth find a way through the seemingly impenetrable Blue Mountains in NSW, opening up the west of the state to settlement.

1851   The discovery of gold near Bathurst, west of the Blue Mountains, almost doubles the population of Sydney within a single decade to around 100,000. The gold rush in Victoria proves even more lucrative and the social and economic focus shifts south.

1859   Queensland becomes a separate colony with its own parliament.

1860–90   Settlement continues in earnest and is largely successful, but the problems of racial disharmony and the sad disintegration of the Aboriginals and their culture remain a major national challenge. From the 1860s until 1969, around 100,000 Aboriginal children are taken from their families and made wards of state.

1901   Federation and the creation of the Commonwealth of Australia.

1927–50   Canberra, the nation's new capital, is established. Almost one million Australians serve in World War II. Immigration

An Aboriginal protest sign outside Old Parliament House, Canberra

increases rapidly. The first of Sydney's two famous icons – the Sydney Harbour Bridge – is completed in 1932. With the discovery of the aqualung, the great 'barrier' of the Barrier Reef is overcome. Cairns' fate as a major international tourist destination is sealed.

1950–70 The infant nation struggles to find its own identity and disenfranchise itself from its colonial past. Aboriginals are granted the vote and are included in census figures.

1973 With the completion of the Opera House, Sydney is well on course to becoming one of the best-loved and most dynamic cities in the world.

1988 Sydney celebrates its bicentennial in the shadow of Aboriginal protest.

1993 The 2000 Olympic Games are awarded to Sydney.

1998 A referendum on a proposal to make Australia a republic is defeated.

2000 The 2000 Olympics prove a great success and are lauded as the best ever. As a result, Australia's global reputation is greatly enhanced.

2001   Australian government pledges almost unbridled support for the United States after the terrorist attack by Al-Qaeda on 11 September and commits troops to the invasion of Iraq.

2002   The nation mourns as 88 of its citizens are killed in a nightclub bombing in Bali, Indonesia. The attack, by radical Islamist group Jemaah Islamiyah, is dubbed Australia's 'September 11'.

2005   Racially motivated violence, involving thousands of youths, hits Sydney. Despite widespread concern, it is passed off as an inevitable symptom – and minor aberration – of a developing cosmopolitan immigrant population.

2006   With the country in the grip of the worst drought on record, the government slashes economic growth forecasts, reflecting a slump in farm output. John Howard declares water security to be Australia's biggest challenge, but still dismisses the Kyoto Climate Change Protocol and joins the US in its refusal to sign.

FAMOUS CONTEMPORARY AUSTRALIAN WOMEN

From pop divas and feminists to A-list actors and Olympians, even comic alter egos, Australia has her fair share of iconic contemporary women.

Love them or hate them, everyone is familiar with the catchy hits of pop princess Kylie Minogue. Fame came at an early age for Kylie, who acted on the popular Australian TV soap *Neighbours* before embarking on a highly successful solo music career. Almost the complete antithesis is Germaine Greer, an internationally recognised author and renowned feminist. Her groundbreaking *The Female Eunuch* became an international best seller in 1970. She lives in the UK but continues to hit the headlines in Australia for her often outspoken, controversial opinions. Other famous contemporaries include actress Nicole Kidman and Aboriginal Olympian Cathy Freeman.

2007   With the Iraq debacle still playing out, climate change a major election issue and despite a booming resource-driven economy, Prime Minister John Howard suffers an embarrassing election defeat. The Australian public look to fresh policy direction and a more youthful leadership in the form of Labor leader and Prime Minister Kevin Rudd.

2008   Rudd gives a formal parliamentary apology to Aboriginal Australians and the 'Stolen Generations'.

Politics

Since federation in 1901, Australia has maintained a stable democratic political system and remains a Commonwealth Realm. The capital city and seat of federal government is in Canberra, located in the Australian Capital Territory.

Due to the relatively young age of Australian politics, its history is not complex, but its structure is. Symbolic executive power is vested in the British monarch, who is represented throughout Australia by the governor-general.

The bicameral parliament consists of the queen, the senate (the upper house) and a house of representatives (the lower house).

Elections for both chambers are held every three years and voting is compulsory. There are three major political parties: the Liberal Party, the Australian Labor Party, and the National Party.

Which party, or where's the party?

The foreign image of Australians as notoriously laid-back and ardent lovers of their enviable and seemingly uncomplicated outdoor lifestyle, together with the fact of a complex political system, has given rise to the perception that the vast majority of the bronzed and contented populace could not care less about politics. Indeed, as long as everyone has a fair go, beer is brewed, surf's up and the nation's heroic cricket team is belting all-comers out of the park, 'why the bloody hell' would you?

Luckily then, perhaps (for the politicians anyway), voting in Australia is compulsory, otherwise turn-out at elections would be something akin to a 'barbie' (BBQ) at Mawson (Australia's base in Antarctica).

Although there is perhaps some truth in this perception, Australians are undoubtedly becoming increasingly 'interested' in politics. There is considerable debate as to why this may be so, but several factors seem to have broken the indifference and threatened the abiding sense of comfort.

The Australian coat of arms above New Parliament House, Canberra

Undoubtedly, the debacle in Iraq plays a part. Increasingly, Australians feel some accountability is due and that the threat of terrorism in Australia and worldwide is increasing, not decreasing as some politicians would vehemently proclaim. In the middle of the worst drought on record and with bush fires worsening in severity and scale, climate change is also a big issue. Additionally, the real estate and rental markets, especially in Sydney, have created a widening gap between young and old, rich and poor. The new social monikers are 'credit crunch' and 'mortgage stress'. All this equates to a concerted desire for change.

In 2007, that change came, predictably, yet dramatically, with the ousting of the Howard government after 11 solid years in power. But whether Labor's relatively youthful leader and polished PM Kevin Rudd can turn down the heat at the political BBQ remains to be seen.

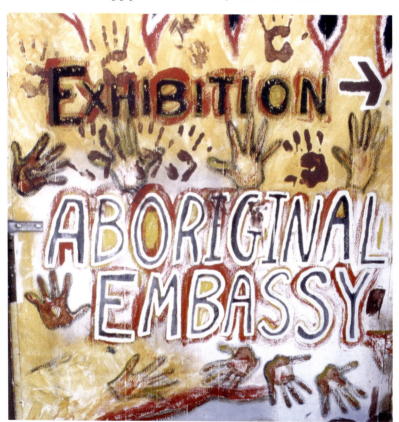

Part of the unofficial, makeshift Aboriginal embassy, Canberra

Culture

Australia is often accused – especially by its colonial bedrock, England – of having two types of desert. One is outback and under oceanic skies; the other is cultural and has showers of beer. Of course, although in decades past this affectionate if provocative label may have held some truth, the reality is that for a country pretty isolated, with only 21 million people and with such a young (white) history, the culture is not only thriving, but world class.

That said, it is very important to note that Australia is (or was), of course, also home to one of the most impressive, complex and long-established cultures on earth: the Aboriginal. Though much of that culture is now lost, or presented in a highly commercial fashion, it is nonetheless well worth investigating deeper while you are there. In many ways our modern culture is ephemeral compared to theirs and its sustainability suspect.

Even a summary of Aboriginal culture is beyond the scope of this book. Suffice to say that its very existence was tried and tested over many thousands of years, resulting in great complexity, although in some ways it is remarkable for its utter simplicity. Above all, until white colonisation, it was sustainable. Unlike our modern culture of music, art and language, the indigenous culture was intrinsic to everyday life, communication and evolution. It was not so much focused on mere entertainment and personal or group creativity as on a vital element of community and long-term survival. In many ways it was their lifeblood.

Music

Australia has a quality classical music and operatic scene, with the Opera House the showcase venue for

Matchsticks by Sydney artist Brett Whiteley

Didgeridoos abound in Sydney's many souvenir shops

the country's top orchestras and performers. When it comes to contemporary popular music, Australia has played its part over recent decades, with INXS, AC/DC and Midnight Oil all being household names. Then there is pop diva Kylie Minogue, who has certainly come a long way from playing 'Charlene' in the popular Australian soap *Neighbours*. And unforgettable, too, were Men at Work, who in 1981 brought us Australia's second and unofficial national anthem, the hopelessly catchy 'Down Under'.

Dance

The Sydney Dance Company was founded in 1969 and, through the solid directorship of resident choreographer Graeme Murphy since 1976, it has become Australia's premier contemporary dance company and one of the country's most prolific and celebrated arts organisations. To date, it has had over 20 highly successful international tours.

Formed in 2001, the Bangarra Dance Theatre, also based in Sydney, is world-renowned for its impressive blend of traditional Aboriginal and Torres Strait Island history and culture with international contemporary dance.

Film

Although born in the US, Mel Gibson grew up in Australia and is recognised by most as an Australian. His roles in such classics as *Mad Max*, *Lethal Weapon* and *Braveheart* made him a household name. Paul Hogan (aka *Crocodile Dundee*) also caused something of a phenomenon in 1986. But their prominence has now been overshadowed in no uncertain terms by the two acting greats Nicole Kidman and Russell Crowe.

Festivals and events

With a climate highly conducive to outdoor activities and a population largely based in coastal cities, Australia enjoys a rich and varied schedule of festivals and events. Most take place in the summer months and a great deal involve Australians' two great loves: sports and the beach. Many are well-established, high-profile annual events, while others are more low-key and localised, often simply celebrating some of life's great pleasures like food, wine or music.

Sport and the great venues

Naturally, Sydney and Brisbane are the focus for the most popular high-profile sports events, and their venues are globally iconic. In Sydney, **Stadium Australia** (*www.anzstadium.com.au*) has seen many a great sporting event since its first role in the 2000 Olympics, and the historic **Sydney Cricket Ground** (*www.sydneycricketground.com.au*) has a rich history. Further north it is 'The

Bondi beach hosts several events throughout the year

Gabba' or **Brisbane Cricket Ground** (*www.thegabba.org.au*) that frequently roars to life with the cry of 'Aussie! Aussie! Aussie!'

Everyone knows that Australians are very keen on cricket and every summer there is an intense schedule of matches in both cities. In winter, Australian Rules Football (*www.afl.com.au*), Rugby Union (*www.rugby.com.au*), Rugby League (*www.nrl.com.au*) and to a lesser extent football (soccer) (*www.footballaustralia.com.au*) predominate.

Culture and history

With a relatively infant colonial (non-Aboriginal) history, Australia makes a big thing of memorial days, with **Australia Day** on 26 January a firm favourite. On that day the flags and face paint, picnics and stubbies (beers) are seemingly omnipresent, with Sydney always stealing the show thanks to its vast flotilla of boats out on the harbour, including the magnificent 'tall ships'.

The 'other races' held annually on Australia Day in Brisbane

Another classic is the colourful **Sydney Gay and Lesbian Mardi Gras** (*www.mardigras.org.au*) held every February. Although many events are involved, the highlight is definitely the parade, where the city's proud and extrovert gay community put on a spectacular show.

Arts and music are a staple in the annual events calendar and be they the majors like the **Sydney Festival** (*www.sydneyfestival.org.au*) or more localised like the **Blues and Roots Festival** (*www.bluesfest.com.au*) in Byron Bay, they are always of high quality, with an impressive international attendance.

Life's a beach

Not surprisingly, many events and festivals are held on the East Coast's abundant beaches. On Bondi Beach in Sydney, both **Christmas** and **New Year** usually prove messy affairs, while in September the **Festival of the Winds** (a kite festival) at the same location is far more sedate. Elsewhere, just about every major beach and surf life-saving club up and down the coast will host some event or other, from the **Australian Surf Life Saving or Surfing Competitions** on the Gold Coast to local **dragon boat races** in Yeppoon.

The other races

Of course Australia would not be Australia if, littered liberally throughout its rich and varied list of annual events, there was not the odd eyebrow raiser. Two in particular stand out and both are in Brisbane. How about attending the annual **Australia Day Cockroach Races** (*www.storybridgehotel.com.au*)? No? Well never mind, save your energy for a spot of **frozen chicken bowling** instead. Well, they do say Queenslanders are 'as mad as cut snakes'!

Highlights

Page	
28	Sydney City
46	NSW North Coast
64	Gold Coast
72	Brisbane City
82	Sunshine & Fraser Coasts
94	Capricorn & Central Queensland Coasts
108	Cairns & Far North

Coral Sea

Kowanyama
Hope Vale
Cooktown
Cape Tribulation
Daintree
CAIRNS
Cairns
Chillagoe
Fitzroy Island
Karumba
Tully
Hinchinbrook Island
Croydon
Greenvale
Orpheus Island
QUEENSLAND
Townsville International
TOWNSVILLE
Cloncurry
Richmond
Collinsville
Mount Dalrymple 1277
Mackay
Corfield
Stamford
Mount Coolon
Winton
Moranbah
Oxford Downs
Barcaldine
Emerald
Rockhampton
Stonehenge
Gladstone
Heron Island
Lady Musgrave Island
Springsure
Biloela
Lady Elliot Island
Yaraka
Caldervale
Fraser Island
Windorah
Taroom
Maryborough
Tin Can Bay
Charleville
Gympie
Tewantin
Roma
Brisbane International
Innamincka
BRISBANE
Thargomindah
Cunnamulla
Toowoomba
Gold Coast
Tibooburra
Goodooga
Murwillumbah
Milparinka
Walgett
Grafton
Byron Bay
Dorrigo
Coffs Harbour
Armidale
Bellingen
Broken Hill
Merrygoen
Mount Barrington 1585
South West Rocks
Port Macquarie
NEW SOUTH WALES
Hermidale
Gloucester
Forster
Darling
Newcastle
Condobolin
Kingsford Smith
Darnick
Katoomba
The Entrance
Griffith
Penrith
SYDNEY
Murrayville
Wollongong
Murray
Tasman Sea
VICTORIA
Culcairn
Canberra
CANBERRA
ACT
GREAT BARRIER REEF

1 **Sydney Harbour** Stunning natural and man-made aesthetics combine to form one of the most beautiful natural harbours in the world. Your first encounter of the iconic Opera House and the Harbour Bridge is guaranteed to last a lifetime.

2 **Blue Mountains** Less than two hours from Sydney CBD, for many visitors the 'Blueys' offer a first taste of two great Australian commodities: 'space' and beautiful national parks.

3 **Myall Lakes NP** After popping a few corks in the Hunter Valley wine region, head here for some solitude, boating, fishing or surfing, or to top up your tan.

4 **South West Rocks** A great stop on the long journey north. After seeing the views from the Smoky Cape Lighthouse and maybe some dolphins in the surf, see how easily one night's stay can turn into three.

5 **Lamington National Park** The 'Green behind the Gold', with its famed rainforest and abundant wildlife, offers the perfect escape from the hype and commercialism of the Gold Coast.

6 **South Bank Brisbane** A golden beach and swimming lagoon in the shadow of the CBD? Say no more.

7 **Fraser Island** Get to grips with a 4WD amid the stunning scenery of the world's largest sand island.

8 **Mon Repos Turtle Rookery** Sit next to these magnificent, ancient creatures as they dig a burrow and lay their eggs, or see the epitome of the phrase 'as keen as baby turtle'.

9 **Hinchinbrook Island** A ruggedly unspoilt island of forested mountain slopes and remote, pristine beaches, home to one of the best multi-day walks in the country.

10 **Diving the Reef** Immerse yourself in that incredible, colourful and hectic world beneath the waves.

The idyll of Lake McKenzie on Fraser Island, Queensland

Suggested itineraries

Given the size of Australia combined with the fact you have already spent considerable time and money just getting there, time is of the essence. But do not make the grave mistake of trying to do too much with the time you have, or it will inevitably turn into an exercise in frustration. Australia as a whole – and the East Coast in particular – simply has too much to offer. It takes Australians months, sometimes years, to discover their own country, so don't for a minute think you can comprehensively do the job in a matter of days or weeks. The following offers a sample of the '101 things you must do' – but without any of that dying nonsense!

Long weekend

Sydney is where it's at.

Day 1 Start with the sunrise at Macquarie Point (harbourside), and then explore the Botanical Gardens, the Opera House, Circular Quay, The Rocks and the Harbour Bridge. After all that activity, rest your feet over a beer in the Lord Nelson pub followed by dinner down at the quay.

Day 2 First a visit to the zoo, then a dip at Balmoral Beach, or the eclectic sights of Darling Harbour, followed by

The Tall Ships Race, Australia Day, Sydney

some retail therapy along George Street. For the more energetic, try the famed 'Bridge Climb'. In the evening, try your luck at the casino or take in a performance at the Opera House.

Day 3 Head to Bondi Beach, taking in the clifftop walk to Bronte, or escape the crowds with a harbour walk from Cremorne to Bradley's Head. Not into walking? Then take the ferry to Manly. In the evening, head to Doyle's Restaurant in Watson's Bay, or watch the sun set over the city from North Head.

One to two weeks

A trip of one or two weeks could only ever sample a specific area between Sydney to Cairns, as well as the two prime destinations in themselves.

After the above long weekend in Sydney, add two or three days exploring the Blue Mountains, the Hunter Valley vineyards, or the Myall Lakes National Park. Then jump on a plane to the Gold Coast and Brisbane, allowing four or five days including an extended trip to either Byron Bay, the hinterland national parks of the Gold Coast and (from Brisbane) Moreton Island or North Stradbroke Islands, or Noosa. Also consider two or three days on Fraser Island.

Then it's back on the plane to Cairns and the Barrier Reef. These could occupy anyone for months, never mind a few days. However, the 'must see and dos' include a reef island trip with snorkelling or an introductory dive, Kuranda and the rainforest gondola,

Looking out from North Stradbroke Island, off the Gold Coast

Daintree, Cape Tribulation, and the perfect retreat from the coastal heat, the Atherton Tablelands.

Longer

If you have three weeks or more, other specific recommended destinations along the East Coast include the following:

• Between Sydney and Brisbane: Port Stephens; Bellingen (including the Dorrigo and New England national parks); Iluka and the Byron Bay hinterland.

• Between Brisbane and Cairns: the Blackall Range from Noosa, Bundaberg; 1770 and Agnes Water, Yeppoon and Great Keppel Island; Airlie Beach and the Whitsunday Islands; Magnetic Island off Townsville; a trip outback to Charters Towers from Townsville; Mission Beach and Dunk Island; and from Cairns that reef classic, Lizard Island.

After all that you will need a holiday!

Australian wildlife

Wildlife is very much part of the Australian holiday experience. Living icons like the koala and kangaroo are as much ingrained in our psyche as the Opera House or Uluru. The great island nation is blessed with one of the richest biodiversities on earth. A volume of species reads like a who's who of the well-known, the utterly spectacular and the 'you've got to be joking'. Best of all, you do not have to venture far to experience it. Indeed, it happens almost by default. Be it a flock of cockatoos over the motorway in Sydney or dolphins surfing beneath the waves in Byron Bay, your encounters will be many and varied and you will inevitably have your own tales to tell.

The icons

The koala (drop the word bear – it's a misnomer) is considered the epitome of all that is cute and cuddly. Koalas eat only eucalyptus leaves and have evolved to fill that very specialist niche. Of course, eating leaves does not require much brainpower, hence they have brains about the size of a walnut and move very slowly. Eucalyptus leaves take a long time to digest, too, which is why koalas could sleep for Australia!

Kangaroos replace the cute and cuddly with brilliance and novelty in design. All roos (except the tree kangaroo) are perfectly adapted for speed. They have evolved to conserve a remarkable amount of energy in motion, with their thick tails acting as a counterbalance.

Both koalas and eastern grey kangaroos are common on the East Coast and there are many excellent zoos and native wildlife sanctuaries where you can get up close and personal with them. Most have displays where you can hold a koala and have the obligatory picture taken.

The beautiful and the bizarre

In their wildest imaginings, Peter Jackson, Damien Hirst and Charles

Koalas spend a lot of time asleep

The mighty Australian 'Saltie' (saltwater crocodile), common in northern Queensland

Darwin still could not have come up with some of the most bizarre Australian species. Who on earth, for example, can look at a platypus without dropping their jaw, or watch a roo hop without tilting their head and thinking, how come? Then there is the Great Barrier Reef, home of the 'Old Wife', the 'Bucket Mouth' and the 'Stone Fish', surely the ugliest face on the planet. And to top that, few people are aware that the reef itself is a living thing, the biggest on the planet, and that it reproduces on just one night every year, around the full moon, in one mass, spectacular orgasm.

And the nasties?

Yes, it is true – there are many dangerous species in Australia, and some can kill. The Taipan (snake), for example, could take out a small household, and shark attacks do occur. But the simple fact of the matter is that the vast majority have absolutely no desire to make your acquaintance, and with a modicum of common sense, you will not be bitten, mauled, or carried off into the sunset shouting 'Croikey'!

Sydney

In the modern age of media hype and global marketing excess, Australia's largest and most celebrated city is one of a decreasing number of iconic destinations that actually lives up to its glowing reputation. You would be hard pressed to find anybody who has made its acquaintance and not left a loyal friend. While Paris and London have their culture and history, and New York its sheer scale, the key to Sydney's winning formula is without doubt its natural beauty and climate.

With much of the city built around a vast, complex natural harbour and its entire eastern flank one long urban oceanfront, the setting could hardly be more beautiful. Add to that a near perfect climate and the instantly recognisable icons of the Opera House and Harbour Bridge, and there could be nothing more effective in putting Australia on the world map.

With a diverse population of 4 million, the pulse of Sydney is a strong one. It is brash, colourful and happening, even a tad arrogant. Sydney is the country's greatest urban draw and the principal gateway to the East Coast, and as such, tourism plays a fundamentally important role in the city's economy.

For the tourist Sydney offers a veritable wealth of things to see and do, many of which are fully deserving of that over-used 'world-class' label. It boasts all the usual suspects – top-quality restaurants, retail outlets, historical and cultural sights and attractions – but it also offers more unusual possibilities, like the Harbour Bridge Climb (*see p38*), stunning harbour walks (*see pp32–3*), and its fair share of great annual festivals like the colourful Gay and Lesbian Mardi Gras.

For more information and bookings contact the **Sydney Visitor Centre** (*Level 1, corner of Argyle St & Playfair St, The Rocks. Tel: 1800 067 676 & (02) 9240 8788. www.therocks.com.au. Open: 9.30am–5.30pm*).

If there is one criticism to be levelled at Sydney, it is its size and all the social and logistical problems that come with it. While it is hardly as manic as Tokyo or Shanghai, this is not a city for the faint-hearted, as getting from A to B can be an ordeal. That said, the public transport system, which combines bus, train and ferry services, is well set up for visitors, with various discounted and combination fare structures. For information about all public transport, contact the **Transport Infoline** (*Tel: 131500. www.131500.com.au*).

Sydney

N

0   200 metres
0   200 yards

Luna Park

Taronga Zoo, Manly & North Head

MILSONS POINT

Stanton Lookout

Milsons Point

KIRRIBILLI

Kirribilli House

Henry Lawson Avenue

BLUES POINT ROAD

Macmahons Point Wharf

Blues Point Reserve

Blues Point

Admiralty House

SYDNEY HARBOUR BRIDGE

SYDNEY HARBOUR TUNNEL

Port Jackson

M ......Metro Monorail
† ......Cathedral
i ......Information
🅟 ......Police Station
🚉 ......Railway Stn
🚌 ......Bus Station
✚ ......Hospital

Wharf Theatre

DAWES POINT

Harbour Bridge Exhibition

Campbells Cove

Sydney Opera House

BRADFIELD HIGHWAY

HICKSON ROAD

LOWER FORT STREET

GEORGE STREET

THE ROCKS

Sydney Cove

Government House

Macquarie Point

Mrs Macquarie's Chair

Lord Nelson

Windmill Street

Rocks Discovery Museum

Museum of Contemporary Art

Sydney Cove

Observatory Park

ARGYLE STREET

Sydney Observatory

MILLERS POINT

KENT STREET

HICKSON ROAD

CUMBERLAND STREET

HARRINGTON STREET

Circular Quay Station

Circular Quay

MACQUARIE STREET

Farm Cove

CAHILL EXPRESSWAY

Customs House

ALFRED STREET

Justice & Police Museum

Museum of Sydney

Conservatorium of Music

Royal Botanic Gardens

The Domain

Andrew 'Boy' Charlton Swimming Pool

GROSVENOR ST

BRIDGE STREET

JAMISON STREET

MARGARET STREET

BOND ST

BENT ST

O'CONNELL STREET

PITT STREET

PHILLIP STREET

LOFTUS STREET

YOUNG STREET

Darling Harbour

WESTERN DISTRIBUTOR

SUSSEX STREET

Wynyard Station

YORK STREET

GEORGE STREET

HUNTER STREET

MACQUARIE STREET

State Library of New South Wales

NSW Parliament House

Sydney Hospital

The Domain

National Maritime Museum

Sydney Wildlife World

Sydney Aquarium

Harbourside

Darling Park

SYDNEY

CLARENCE STREET

KENT STREET

KING STREET

Martin Place Station

Martin Place

Sydney Mint Museum

Sydney Tower

Hyde Park Barracks

Art Gallery of New South Wales

ART GALLERY ROAD

COWPER WHARF ROADWAY

WOOLLOOMOOLOO WHARF

WOOLLOOMOOLOO

NICHOLSON STREET

BROUGHAM STREET

i

Harbourside

Convention Station

Imax Theatre

MARKET ST

Queen Victoria Building

Galeries Victoria

City Centre

ST JAMES RD

Archibald Fountain

St James Station

St Mary's Cathedral

CATHEDRAL STREET

Elizabeth Bay House

KINGS CROSS

Kings Cross Station

DARLINGHURST ROAD

Sydney Fish Market

DARLING HARBOUR

St Andrew's Cathedral

Town Hall

Town Hall Station

DRUITT ST

PARK ST

Hyde Park

WILLIAM STREET

YURONG STREET

CROWN STREET

PREMIER LANE

Watson's Bay & South Head

BATHURST ST

ELIZABETH STREET

Museum Station

Australian Museum

FRANCIS LANE

PALMER STREET

BOURKE STREET

Exhibition Centre Station

Chinese Garden of Friendship

HARBOUR STREET

PIER STREET

Anzac War Memorial

LIVERPOOL STREET

COLLEGE STREET

DARLINGHURST

OXFORD STREET

BURTON STREET

LIVERPOOL STREET

Powerhouse Museum

Paddy's Market

CHINATOWN

World Square

GOULBURN ST

WENTWORTH AVENUE

CASTLEREAGH STREET

GOULBURN STREET

FOLEY STREET

Paddy's Market Station

HAYMARKET

HARRIS STREET

MARY ANN ST

Capitol Square Station

GEORGE STREET

PITT STREET

CAMPBELL STREET

SURRY HILLS

COMMONWEALTH STREET

RESERVOIR STREET

CROWN STREET

OXFORD STREET

PADDINGTON

BOUNDARY STREET

Sydney Coach Terminal

Central Railway Station

Brett Whiteley Museum & Gallery

Moore Park, SCG & Centennial Park

Bondi Beach

Beat that and there really is only one overriding problem left for the average overseas visitor: the paucity of time you inevitably have to experience the place. Pre-planning is therefore important. Don't make the common mistake of extending your stay in Sydney to the detriment of the rest of the East Coast. Bear in mind that this is just the area's urban offerings. Out there is an even more impressive natural world awaiting your acquaintance. This is just the start.

Circular Quay and The Rocks
Museum of Contemporary Art

Located between Circular Quay and The Rocks, the grand Art Deco Museum of Contemporary Art houses a collection of some of Australia's best modern works, together with works by renowned international artists such as Warhol and Hockney. The museum also hosts regular national and international exhibitions. The in-house café overlooking the quay is also popular.

140 George St, The Rocks.
Tel: (02) 9241 5892. www.mca.com.au.
Open: daily 10am–5pm. Tours: Mon–Fri
11am & 2pm, Sat & Sun noon &
1.30pm. Free admission. Ferry, bus &
train: Circular Quay.

The Rocks

The Rocks village was the first site settled by European convicts and troops as early as 1788 and is the oldest part of the city. It was once the haunt of prostitutes, drunks and criminals, but although its social fabric has certainly changed, it still retains much of its original architectural charm. The area now serves as one of Sydney's most popular attractions, with an eclectic array of shops, galleries, arcades, cafés, old pubs and restaurants.

Sydney Harbour Bridge, with the Opera House in the distance

The popular **Rocks Market** (*George St & Playfair St, The Rocks. Open: Sat & Sun 10am–5pm*) features contemporary arts, crafts and souvenirs. The 90-minute **Rocks Walking Tour** is an excellent way to learn about the torrid history of the area (*Tours depart from 23 Playfair St, The Rocks. Tel: (02) 9247 6678. www.rockswalkingtours.com.au*).

Nearby in Kendal Lane, the **Rocks Discovery Museum** (*Tel: (02) 9251 8804. www.rocksdiscoverymuseum.com.au. Open: 10am–5pm. Free admission*) houses interactive historical exhibits.

To escape the crowds and see some fine views, head up Argyle St to **Observatory Park**, which is also home to the **Sydney Observatory** (*Tel: (02) 9921 3485. www.sydneyobservatory.com.au. Admission charge*), Australia's oldest, where tours are available.

Sydney Harbour Bridge

Affectionately nicknamed 'The Coathanger', the Sydney Harbour Bridge is one of the greatest urban constructions in the world. Opened in 1932, having taken nine years to build and reaching 134m (440ft) in height, it supports eight lanes of traffic (accommodating up to 175,000 vehicles a day), a railway line and a pedestrian walkway. Until recently, the best views from the bridge were accessed by foot from its 59m-high (194ft) deck, but now the 'Bridge Climb' experience has become a world-famous Sydney 'must-do' (*see p38*).

There are also (far cheaper) views on offer from the top of the southeastern Pylon Lookout, accessed from the eastern walkway and Cumberland St, The Rocks. The pylon also houses the **Harbour Bridge Exhibition** (*Open: 10am–5pm. Tel: (02) 9247 3408. Admission charge*). From below, the best views of the bridge can be enjoyed from Hickson Rd and Dawes Point Park (south side) and Milsons Point (north side).

Sydney Opera House

Completed in 1973 and now arguably Australia's most recognised (man-made) icon, the Sydney Opera House cannot fail to impress. Its intriguing, shell-like façades house five performance venues ranging from the main 2,690-capacity Concert Hall to the small Playhouse Theatre. Combined, they host about 2,500 performances annually. The Opera House is the principal performance venue for Opera Australia, the Australian Ballet, the Sydney Symphony Orchestra and the Sydney Theatre Company. Bookings for tours, performances and packages are essential and available online. Cafés, bars, a restaurant and a store are also located within the complex. On summer evenings the bars below the main complex must surely be one of the best places on the planet for a convivial beer or G&T.
Via Macquarie St, Circular Quay. Tel: (02) 9250 7777. www.soh.nsw.gov.au. Open: Mon–Sat 9am–8.30pm. Free admission, tours extra. Ferry, bus & train: Circular Quay.

Harbour walk: Cremorne to Balmoral Beach

This walk offers some stunning views of Sydney's vast natural harbour, and a swim or lunch at Balmoral Beach provides the perfect end.

Allow 5–6 hours for the 11.5km (7 miles). Alternatively, split the walk into two: allow 3 hours for Taronga Zoo to Balmoral (6.5km/4 miles), and 2–3 hours for Cremorne to Taronga Zoo (5km/3 miles).

It is best to start the full walk at Cremorne (access by bus or ferry) and the half walk at Taronga Zoo (lower entrance, also accessed by bus or ferry). For all transport enquiries, contact **Transport Infoline** *(Tel: 131 500.*

www.131500.com.au). A Greater Sydney map is also recommended.

1 Cremorne Point

From the entrance of Cremorne Reserve on Bogota Ave (off Milson Rd),

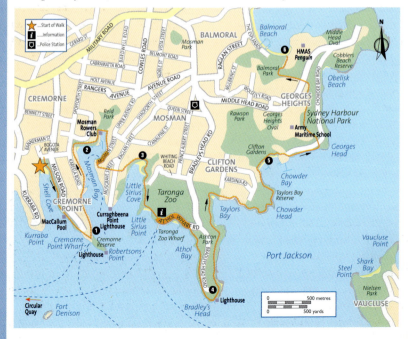

walk to **Cremorne Point Lighthouse**, past the idyllic **MacCallum Pool** and Cremorne Point Wharf, pausing to take in the spectacular views across to the Opera House.

From there, continue alongside Mosman Bay to the Mosman Rowers Club, past the stunning real estate.

2 Mosman Bay

Mosman is one of the most prestigious suburbs in the city, with real estate average prices over A$1 million.

From Mosman Bay Wharf, climb the steps to Mosman St. Turning right, continue to McLeod St, then head due east down the steps to Little Sirius Cove.

3 Little Sirius Cove and Taronga Zoo

Continue round the peaceful Little Sirius Cove and alongside the zoo boundary to the Taronga Zoo Wharf. Look out for bearded dragons (a harmless type of lizard and not as odious as the name suggests) sunning themselves along the path.

From the Zoo Wharf, head along Athol Wharf Rd past the zoo's lower entrance and rejoin the coastal path to Bradley's Head.

4 Bradley's Head

Bradley's Head has been a lookout for years and was doubtless used as such by the local Aboriginals, who called it Dalyungay, meaning 'a place of surveillance, look-out or alarm'. Note the twisted trunks of the **Sydney Red Gums**.

From the point, continue through the bush reserve, past Taylors Bay and Chowder Head to Chowder Bay.

5 Chowder Bay and Georges Heights

From the beach at Chowder Bay walk up the wooden steps into the former **Army Maritime School**. Naval vessels are often moored here. The walkway continues through the complex (signposted) to Georges Heights. This stretch offers some excellent views out towards North and South Heads and across to the eastern suburbs.

From Georges Heights, descend the stairs to Balmoral Park and Balmoral Beach.

6 Balmoral Beach

This is one of the city's most beautiful beaches and due to its location does not suffer the same attention as Bondi or its other oceanside counterparts. It is a great place for a swim, and beachside cafés and restaurants add some sophistication.

From here you can catch a bus back to Circular Quay (via Mosman) or Taronga Zoo Wharf.

The view towards 'The Heads' from Balmoral, Sydney

City centre

Hyde Park and surrounds

Located alongside the Central Business District and graced with spacious lawns and mighty corridors of trees, Hyde Park is a magnet for city suits at lunchtime. The 1932 **Archibald Fountain** and 1934 **Anzac War Memorial** are its main historical features. Nearby stands the impressive **St Mary's Cathedral**. Free tours run on Sunday afternoons after midday mass (*College St. Tel: (02) 9220 0400. Free admission. Explorer bus: stop 5*).

The **Australian Museum**, established in 1827, is well up with the play of technology, presentation and entertainment, with the biodiversity and indigenous Australian displays being of particular note. Children are also well catered for in the state-of-the-art 'Search and Discover' section and 'Kidspace', a mini museum for the under 5s (*6 College St. Tel: (02) 9320 6000. www.austmus.gov.au. Open: 9.30am–5pm. Admission charge, and special exhibitions extra. Explorer bus: stop 6*).

Macquarie Street

Along with The Rocks, Macquarie is the historical hub of the city and retains many of its most significant and impressive colonial buildings.

From north to south, the first, surrounded by its own expansive grounds, is the 1837 **Government House**. The interior contains many period furnishings and features giving an insight into the lifestyle of the former

The Museum of Sydney, dwarfed by modern high-rises

NSW governors and their families (*Tel: (02) 9931 5222. Open: Fri–Sun 10am–3pm, grounds 10am–4pm. Free admission & guided tours*).

Further along is the **State Library of New South Wales**, housing some very significant historical documents, including eight out of the ten known First Fleet diaries, as well as visiting exhibitions. There's a shop and café on site (*Tel: (02) 9273 1414. www.slnsw.gov.au. Open: Mon–Fri 9am–9pm, Sat & Sun 11am–5pm. Admission charge for visiting exhibitions*).

Next door to the library is the **NSW Parliament House**. Free tours are available when parliament is not in session (*www.parliament.nsw.gov.au*).

The former 1816 **Hyde Park Barracks** lie on the northern fringe of Hyde Park and now house a modern museum displaying their history and

the work of the architect Francis Greenway. Tours are available and there's a café on site.
Macquarie St. Tel: (02) 9223 8922. www.hht.nsw.gov.au. Open: 9.30am–5pm. Admission charge. Explorer bus: stop 4.

Museum of Sydney

Built on the original site of Governor Phillip's (the captain of the 'First Fleet') former 1788 residence, the MOS explores the history and stories that surround the creation and development of the city. Shop and café on site.
37 Phillip St. Tel: (02) 9251 5988. www.hht.nsw.gov.au. Open: 9.30am–5pm. Admission charge.

Queen Victoria Building (QVB)

Taking up an entire city block, the grand Queen Victoria Building was built in 1898 to celebrate Queen Victoria's Golden Jubilee. Amid the ornate architecture, stained-glass windows, mosaics and two charming and intricate Automata Turret Clocks are three floors of modern boutique

outlets, galleries, restaurants and cafés.
455 George St. Tel: (02) 9267 4761. www.qvb.com.au. Open: daily, guided tours twice daily (Tel: (02) 9264 9209). Explorer bus: stop 14.

Sydney (Centrepoint) Tower

Rising from the heart of the Central Business District, the 250m (820ft) Sydney Tower has, since 1981, been an instantly recognisable landmark across the city. As well as the expansive vistas from the tower's **Observation Deck** (*Open: Sun–Fri 9am–10.30pm, Sat 9am–11.30pm. Admission charge*), you can also experience a virtual 'Great Australian Expedition' tour (*Extra admission charge*), or dine in one of two revolving restaurants. The more adventurous can even venture outdoors and experience **Skywalk**, a glass-floored platform (*Open: 9.30am–8.45pm. Tel: (02) 9333 9200. www.skywalk.com.au. Admission charge*).
100 Market St. Tel: (02) 9231 9300, restaurant bookings (02) 8223 3800. Explorer bus: stop 14.

Sydney skyline viewed from the Opera House

Darling Harbour and Chinatown

Chinese Garden of Friendship

Offering a little sanctuary from the bustling markets and restaurants of Chinatown, the Garden of Friendship contains all the usual intricate craftsmanship, landscaping and aesthetics. It was gifted to NSW by her sister Chinese province, Guangdong, to celebrate the Australian Bicentenary in 1988. There is also a teahouse (*Open: 10am–4.30pm*).
Southern end of Darling Harbour. Tel: (02) 9240 8888. www.chinesegarden.com.au. Open: 9.30am–5pm. Admission charge. Metro Monorail: Chinatown. LightRail: Paddy's Market. Explorer bus: stop 20. Ferry: from Circular Quay to Darling Harbour.

National Maritime Museum

Offers a fine mix of old and new, in both diversity and scale. Moored alongside the museum, the small warship HMAS *Vampire* and submarine HMAS *Onslow* sit in stark contrast to the beautifully restored 1874 square rigger the *James Craig*, and the replica of Captain Cook's ship of discovery, the *Endeavour*. Inside the museum, a range of displays explore Australia's close links with all things nautical, from the early navigators and the First Fleet to the ocean liners which brought many waves of immigrants, the navy, sport and leisure. There is also a café, shop, sailing lessons and a range of short cruises on a variety of historical vessels.

2 Murray St. Tel: (02) 9298 3777. www.anmm.gov.au. Open: 9.30am–5pm. Admission charge. Monorail: Harbourside. Explorer bus: stop 19. Ferry: from Circular Quay to Darling Harbour.

Powerhouse Museum

Housing nearly 400,000 items collected over 120 years, this remains Australasia's largest museum. The collection focuses on Australian innovation and achievement, and covers a wide range of general topics from science and technology to transportation, social history and design. Shop and café on site.
500 Harris St, Ultimo. Tel: (02) 9217 0111. www.phm.gov.au. Open: 10am–5pm. Admission charge. Monorail and LightRail: Paddy's Market. Explorer bus: stop 17.

Darling Harbour, just a short stroll from Sydney's Central Business District

Sydney Aquarium

Considered the country's best – and it's not all about fish. Its 650-species inventory – showcased in an imaginative array of habitats – includes saltwater crocodiles, frogs, seals, penguins and platypuses. The highlight is the Great Barrier Reef Oceanarium, a huge tank that gives you an incredible insight into the world's largest living thing. Also of note are some of the highly poisonous marine creatures, such as the notorious box jellyfish, the cone shell, and the rockfish.

Aquarium Pier. Tel: (02) 9262 2300.
www.sydneyaquarium.com.au.
Open: 9am–8pm. Admission charge.
Metro Monorail: Harbourside. LightRail:
Convention. Explorer bus: stop 21. Ferry:
from Circular Quay to Darling Harbour.

Sydney Fish Market

Not everybody's fish and chips, but a fine alternative to the more commercial attractions. Every morning at dawn, over 2,500 crates of seafood covering 100 species from coastal New South Wales are sold to a lively bunch of buyers using a computerised auction clock system. Tours of the auction floor, which need to be pre-booked, are available and there are cafés, some excellent seafood eateries and open markets where seafood can be bought at competitive prices.

Bank St, Pyrmont. Tel: (02) 9004 1100.
www.sydneyfishmarket.com.au.
Open: 6am onwards, tours Mon & Thur 7am onwards. Admission charge for tour.

Replica of the tall ship HMS *Bounty*, moored at the Australian National Maritime Museum, Darling Harbour

LightRail: Fish Markets. Bus: 443 (from Circular Quay) or 501 (from Town Hall).

Sydney Wildlife World

The city's newest high-profile tourist attraction offers 65 exhibits hosting 100 native Australian species. There are nine impressive habitat exhibits, including the 'Flight Canyon' and the 'Nocturnal', housing all the usual suspects, from koalas to wallabies.

Aquarium Pier. Tel: (02) 9333 9288.
www.sydneywildlifeworld.com.au.
Open: 9am–10pm. Admission charge.
Monorail: Darling Park. Explorer bus: stop 24. Ferry: from Circular Quay to Darling Harbour.

For more information on Darling Harbour, call or visit the **Harbourside Information Desk** (*Level 2, Harbourside Shopping Centre. Tel: (02) 9281 3999.* *www.darlingharbour.com.au*).

Sydney activities

Harbour Bridge Climb

Without doubt the highest-profile activity in Sydney is the award-winning Bridge Climb, a 3-hour ascent of the 134m (440ft) Harbour Bridge. It can be undertaken day or night and the harbour views are spectacular. Note, however, that for safety reasons you cannot take your own camera on the trip.
5 Cumberland St, The Rocks.
Tel: (02) 8274 7777.
www.bridgeclimb.com.
Open: 7am–7pm. Admission charge.

'Bridge climbers' scale (and provide scale on) the span of the Sydney Harbour Bridge

Harbour cruises

There is a vast array on offer, with most being based at Circular Quay and Darling Harbour. Trips vary from sedate dinner cruises on paddle steamers to scenic trips on fast catamarans and even jet-boat rides. The Sydney Visitor Centre (*see p28*) and Harbourside Information Desk (*see p37*) have details and take bookings. Note that a multiple-trip ferry ticket is a perfectly good and far cheaper alternative.

Sailing

Sydney Harbour offers some of the best sailing in the world.
Sydney Mainsail (*Tel: (02) 9979 3681. www.sydneymainsail.com.au*) offers 3-hour trips several times daily with highly experienced skippers.
Australian Spirit Sailing Company (*Tel: (02) 9878 0300. www.austspiritsailingco.com.au*) and **Sydney by Sail** based at the National Maritime Museum (*Tel: (02) 9280 1110. www.sydneybysail.com*) are two other alternatives, with the latter running social day trips and introductory lessons.

Scenic flights

Both fixed-wing and helicopter scenic flights are available.

Sydney Heli-Aust (*Bankstown Airport. Tel: (02) 9791 0322. www.heliaust.com.au*) offers pick-ups from the city. **Palm Beach Seaplanes** (*Rose Bay & Palm Beach. Tel: (02) 1300 656 787. www. sydneybyseaplane.com.au*) offers an interesting alternative. Flight times range from 15 to 60 minutes.

There are also some options for the more adventurous, including **Red Baron Scenic Flights** (*Tel: (02) 9791 0643 www. redbaron.com.au*), offering an unforgettable aerobatic scenic harbour flight in an open cockpit. Then there is the antithesis: ballooning. **Cloud 9** (*Tel: 1300 555 711. www.cloud9balloonflights.com*) and **Balloon Aloft** (*Tel: 1800 028 568. www.balloonaloft.com*) both offer early morning flights over the outer suburbs or in the Hunter Valley.

Sea kayaking

The vast harbour lends itself to kayaking and you can literally lose yourself for hours in the many bays and tributaries. Kayaks can be hired from the **Sydney Kayak Centre** (*Spit Rd, Spit Bridge. Tel: (02) 9969 4590*). **Sydney Harbour Kayaks** (*3/235 Spit Rd, Mosman. Tel: (02) 9960 4389. www.sydneyharbourkayaks.com.au*) offers guided trips.

Surfing

Manly and Bondi are the places to hire boards, try to stay upright and have lessons. Try the **Manly Surf School** for good-value, 11am–1pm daily classes (*North Steyne Surf Club, Manly Beach. Tel: (02) 9977 6977. www.manlysurfschool.com*).
In Bondi try the **Bondi Surf Company** (*2/72 Campbell Parade. Tel: (02) 9365 0870*).

Swimming

The ocean beaches at Bondi, Bronte, Clovelly and Coogee are recommended, while to the north, Manly, Collaroy, Narrabeen, Avalon, Ocean Beach and Palm Beach are also good spots. Lifeguards patrol most beaches in summer, but make sure you always swim between the yellow and red flags.

SYDNEY TRAVEL PASSES

The **Day-Tripper Pass** gives all-day access to trains, buses and ferries, and can be purchased at any rail, bus or ferry sales or information outlet or on buses. **Travel Pass** allows unlimited, weekly or quarterly combined travel throughout designated zones or sections. For the tourist, **The Sydney Pass** is a good bet, offering unlimited travel on ferry and standard buses as well as on the Sydney and Bondi Explorer routes and the four STA Harbour Cruises. They are sold as three-day, five-day or seven-day passes. Discount, ten-trip 'Travel Ten' (bus) and 'Ferry Ten' (ferry) passes are also recommended.
Tel: 131 500. www.13150.info

East of the centre
Art Gallery of New South Wales
At the southeastern corner of the Botanical Gardens is this, Australia's largest gallery. Housed behind its grand façade are permanent works of contemporary Australian artists, an impressive international collection and the Yiribana Gallery, dedicated to works by Aboriginals and Torres Strait Islanders. Half-hour dance and music performances add to the experience. *Art Gallery Rd, Domain. Tel: (02) 9225 1744. www.artgallery.nsw.gov.au. Open: 10am–5pm, performances Tue–Sat noon. Free admission. Explorer bus: stop 12.*

Bondi Beach
The most famous of Sydney's many ocean beaches and the epitome of the great Sydney lifestyle. Behind the beach, Bondi's bustling waterfront offers a tourist trap of cafés, restaurants, bars, surf and souvenir shops. To the south, **Bronte Beach** connects with Bondi Beach via a popular scenic clifftop walkway. *Bus: 321, 322, 365, 366, 380 from Circular Quay. Rail: from Circular Quay to Bondi Junction (Illawara Line), then bus (numbers above).*

Eastern suburbs
Situated near the Navy's Woolloomooloo docks, **Kings Cross** (or 'the Cross' as it is nicknamed) has been the hub of the city's nightlife for decades. For some it is totally overrated, but others end up staying there for weeks. There is really only one way to find out if it's your scene.

Located close to the Cross is **Elizabeth Bay House**, a revival-style estate built in 1845 (*7 Onslow Ave, Elizabeth Bay. Tel: (02) 9356 3022. Open: Tue–Sun 10am–4.30pm. Admission charge. Explorer bus: stop 9*). The interior is restored and faithfully furnished in accordance with the times, and the house has a great outlook across the harbour.

Just south of the Cross, **Darlinghurst** and **Surry Hills** offer a wealth of fine restaurants and cafés. In Surry Hills don't miss the **Brett Whiteley Museum and Gallery**, the former studio and home of one of Sydney's most popular contemporary artists, who died in 1992 (*2 Raper St. Tel: (02) 9225 1881. Open: 10am–4pm. Admission charge*).

Sydney's famous Bondi Beach

Sydney's Royal Botanic Gardens contrast with the city office blocks

The big attraction in **Paddington** is **Oxford St**, one of the most happening areas of the city, and a conglomerate of cheap eateries, cafés, restaurants, clubs and bars. It is also a major focus for the city's gay community. The colourful **Paddington Market** is held every Saturday from 10am (*395 Oxford St. Tel: (02) 9331 2923*). Just to the south of Paddington, Moore Park is home to the famous **Sydney Cricket Ground** (*Tours tel: (02) 9380 0383. Explorer bus: stop 16*). Further south again is **Centennial Park**, which at 220ha (540 acres) is Sydney's largest.

Watson's Bay, sitting on the leeward side of South Head, which guards the mouth of Sydney Harbour, offers some fine short walks and historic points of interest and is home to the famous **Doyles Seafood Restaurant** (*Tel: (02) 9337 2007. Ferry: from Circular Quay Wharfs 2 & 4. Bus: 325 & 342 from Circular Quay*).

Royal Botanic Gardens
A short stroll from the city centre, the 30ha (74-acre), 200-year-old Royal Botanic Gardens boast a fine array of mainly native plants and trees, rose and succulent gardens, a Tropical House (*Admission charge*), decorative ponds and a resident colony of flying foxes (bats). There is also a visitor centre, shop, café and restaurant (*Tel: (02) 9231 8050*). From the Botanic Gardens it is a short stroll via Mrs Macquarie's Rd to **Macquarie Point**, which offers one of the best vistas of the Opera House and Harbour Bridge (*Explorer bus: stop 5*).
Art Gallery Rd. Tel: (02) 9231 8111. www.rbgsyd.nsw.gov.au. Open: 7am–sunset. Free admission. Explorer bus: stop 4.

The North Shore and city outskirts

Manly

Manly is more resort than suburb and offers a great day away from the city centre. Its famous surf beach is very much the main attraction, together with a happening restaurant and café scene. The one let-down is its rather tacky 'Corso' pedestrian precinct, but this is now being out-classed by the fast-developing wharf and waterfront areas. Other main tourist attractions are the **Oceanworld** aquarium complex (*Tel: (02) 8251 7877. www.oceanworld.com.au. Open: 10am–5.30pm. Admission charge*) and the **Manly Art Gallery and Museum** (*Tel: (02) 9976 1420. Open: Tue–Sun 10am–5pm. Free admission*), both located just west of the wharf.

A visit to the tip of the **North Head** peninsula (just south of Manly) is very worthwhile, particularly at sunset. The views across the harbour towards the city are spectacular. Just follow Scenic Drive to the very end. The **Quarantine Station** (*Tel: 1300 886 875. www.q-station.com.au. Admission charge for tours*), which takes up a large portion of the peninsula, was used from 1832 to harbour ships known to be carrying diseases like smallpox or bubonic plague. The station closed in 1984 and is now administered as a historical site by the NSW Parks and Wildlife Service. Two-hour tours are available (*Wed–Sat*

Palm Beach, one of many beaches on Sydney's beautiful North Shore

3pm, Sun 10am & 1pm), as are three-hour 'Ghost Tours' (*Wed–Sun 7.30pm*) and two-hour 'Family Tours' (*Thur & Sun 6pm*).

Northern beaches
The coast north of Manly is inundated by picturesque bays and fine surf beaches that stretch 40km (25 miles) to Barrenjoey Head and the mighty Hawkesbury River harbour. Not surprisingly, this area is the location of some extremely sought-after suburban real estate. Perhaps the most popular of the beaches are Narrabeen, Avalon and Whale Beach, but there are many to choose from.

At the very tip is **Barrenjoey Head**, crowned by a historic lighthouse built in 1881. Nearby is the beautiful **Palm Beach**, made famous as the principal filming location for the Aussie soap *Home and Away*. Day cruises up the **Hawkesbury River** or shorter excursions to the **Ku-ring-gai Chase National Park** are available from the **Palm Beach Public Wharf** (*Tel: (02) 9997 4815. Bus: 90 from Wynard to Palm Beach*).

Taronga Zoo
Set harbourside and amid the most expensive real estate in Australia, Taronga can certainly boast one of the best locations and views of any zoo in the world. Going back as far as 1881, the institution is an old one and as such has built up an extensive species list that includes the obligatory koala, platypus, marsupials and colourful

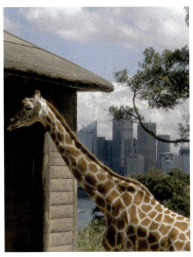
Sydney's Taronga Zoo

Australian birds. The more traditional residents are also in evidence and include gorilla, tiger, bear, giraffe, the largest captive troupe of chimps in the world, and a large new elephant enclosure. You will almost certainly need a full day to explore the various exhibits on offer and there are plenty of events staged throughout the day to keep both adults and children entertained. The best of these is without doubt the Free Flight Bird Show, staged twice daily in an open-air arena overlooking the city.

A Zoo Pass combo ticket includes ferry transfers and zoo entry.
Tel: (02) 9969 2777. www.zoo.nsw.gov.au. Open: 9am–5pm. Admission charge. Ferry: from Circular Quay Wharf 2, every half hour Mon–Fri 7.15am–6.45pm, Sat 8.45am–6.45pm, Sun 8.45am–5.45pm.

Tour: Blue Mountains

Less than two hours' drive west of Sydney, the 'Blueys' (as they are affectionately known) contain five national parks covering a total area of 10,000sq km (3,860sq miles). A network of eroded river valleys, gorges and bluffs offer a vast wonderland of natural features, from precipitous cliffs to dramatic waterfalls. The 'blue' label derives from the visual effects of sunlight on oils released by the vast swathes of eucalyptus forest.

Allow a whole day for the 279km (173-mile) route.

From the centre of Sydney, take the M4 (toll) west to Glenbrook.

1 Glenbrook

Located just beyond the Nepean River, the small village of Glenbrook is considered the gateway to the Blue Mountains. From the northern end of the village follow signs to **Lennox Bridge**, the oldest in Australia, built by convicts in 1833. Nearby **Knapsack Park** offers fine views back towards Sydney, though this is just a taste of better things to come.

From Glenbrook, continue west on the Western Highway (SH32) to Wentworth Falls.

2 Wentworth Falls

The stunning lookouts across **Wentworth Falls** and the **Jamieson Valley** (signposted off SH32) offer a dramatic introduction to the classic scenery of the Blue Mountains. Walking tracks take in viewpoints around the falls, and the **Den Fenella Track** will take you to some good lookouts.
From Wentworth Falls, continue west on the Western Highway (SH32) to Katoomba.

3 Katoomba and around

Considered the capital of the Blue Mountains, the historic town of Katoomba is an interesting mix of old and new, with its tourism highlight being the **Three Sisters** lookout at **Echo Point**, the Blueys' most famous. From the lookout it is possible to walk around to the stacks and descend the taxing **Giant Stairway Walk** to the valley floor (30 minutes). The **Katoomba Visitors Information Centre** is at Echo Point (*Tel: 1300 653 408. www.visitbluemountains.com.au. Open: 9am–5pm*).

West of Echo Point is the highly commercial **Scenic World**, with various unusual scenic transportation opportunities (*junction of Cliff Drive and Violet St. Tel: (02) 4782 2699. www.scenicworld.com.au. Open: 9am–5pm. Admission charge*).

From Katoomba, continue northwest on the Western Highway (SH32) to Blackheath.

4 Blackheath

The sleepy little village of Blackheath is especially popular in autumn when the tree-lined streets turn to gold. But year round it is **Evans** and **Govetts Leap** lookouts that provide the aesthetic drama. An added attraction is **Bridal Veil Falls**, the highest in the Blue Mountains. The lookouts are all signposted from the village.
Continue on SH32 to Mount Victoria then turn right following signs to Bell. At Bell turn left (west) on SH40 to Clarence.

5 Zig Zag Railway and the Bells Line of Road

Clarence forms the terminus of the Zig Zag Railway. Originally built in 1866, restored steam trains now make the 8km (5-mile), 1½-hour journey to Bottom Points (*Tel: (02) 6351 4826. www.zigzagrailway.com.au. Trains depart from Clarence: Wed, Sat & Sun 11am, 1pm & 3pm. Journey fare*).
*Returning east on SH40 (the Bells Line of Road), follow the northern rim of the Grose Valley. This will take you back to Sydney via Richmond and Windsor. The main point of interest is the 28ha (69-acre) cool-climate **Sydney (Mount Tomah) Botanic Garden**, home to over 10,000 species (Tel: (02) 4567 2154. www.rbgsyd.nsw.gov.au. Open: 10am–4pm. Admission charge*).

The New South Wales north coast

Heading north from the vast urban mêlée of Sydney, the bush-clad rocky outcrops of the Ku-ring-gai Chase National Park and undeveloped bays of the Hawkesbury River quickly begin to re-establish that sense of space and nature for which Australia is so well known. You are soon delivered to the green rolling hills of the Hunter Valley, where it would be almost rude not to visit some of the country's most lauded vineyards and sample some of its finest labels.

Many take advantage of the quality accommodation that is so often associated with great wine regions, while others head for the down-to-earth industrial town of Newcastle. The latter is in stark contrast to the valley but has its own historical appeal. Port Stephens offers another fine alternative and, like almost every coastal settlement from here to Cairns, possesses an asset that you will no doubt gladly get used to: beautiful ocean beaches.

From the Hunter Valley, Port Stephens or Newcastle, a day or two exploring the waterways and beaches of the Myall Lakes National Park is a must before experiencing the enviable coastal lifestyle and scenery in Port Macquarie, South West Rocks or Coffs Harbour.

But as with all good things, it's wise to take a break every so often, and inland the alternative arty township of Bellingen, the cool rainforests of the Dorrigo National Park, or the wilderness views within the New England National Park offer the ideal opportunity and can all be combined in a single day (*see pp56–7*).

Beyond Coffs Harbour the small seaside villages of Iluka and Yamba are the gateways to the Bundjalung and Yuraygir National Parks, both of which possess a biodiversity as intriguing as their names. Again, with peace and quiet aplenty, they provide the undeveloped calm before the

Looking south from Cape Hawke to the Myall Lakes National Park

New South Wales north coast

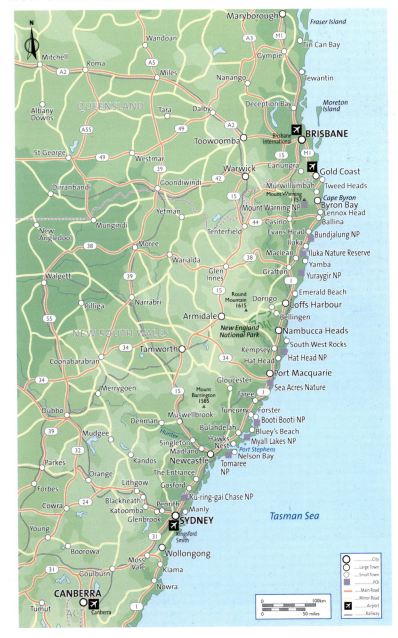

commercial storm that is Byron Bay, the NSW north coast's most celebrated tourist town. It is hard to believe that two decades ago it was just a conglomerate of shacks frequented by laid-back surfers. But like the entire East Coast, it was not long before the near-utopian lifestyle concept caught on, and when the artisans arrived, its fate, like so many others, was sealed. Now a bustling cosmopolitan town, Byron offers everything from simple sunbathing to surfing lessons, so your stay can be as active or inactive as you desire.

Once again, should it all reach overload and you need to touch base with nature, head inland towards the volcanic peak of Mount Warning, which quietly beckons in the background, ancient and unchanged.

Newcastle

167km (104 miles) from Sydney
Newcastle was founded in 1804 as a small penal colony. Vast coal deposits in the Hunter Valley quickly led to it becoming a shipping and commercial centre by the 1860s. Despite recent decline, it is still a major coal port and, with a population of almost half a million, the sixth-largest city in Australia.

Of course, given its primary function, the city is hardly an aesthetic stunner – far from it – but despite the landscape,

The mouth of Port Stephens from Tomaree lookout

it does offer some interesting historical and cultural attractions as well as some of the finest surfing beaches in the state. Indeed, it is a quite a bizarre sight to see surfers riding the waves with a veritable fleet of freighters sitting in the bay behind them, all awaiting their turn to load up the black stuff. It is not unusual to see as many as 50 of the red hulks spread across the horizon. Newcastle is also noted for one particularly ominous and unusual historical event: a major earthquake that struck in 1989 with the loss of 12 lives.

For the best views of the city and coastline, head to the Obelisk on Ordnance St, near the city centre, or **Fort Scratchley**, on Nobby's Rd at the mouth of the harbour. Fort Scratchley also houses the newly restored **Maritime and Military Museum** (*Tel: (02) 4929 3066. www.fortscratchley.org.au*).

The city centre retains some noted historical buildings, including the Christ Church Cathedral (1892), Courthouse (1890) and Customs House (1877). Also worthy of a perusal is the **Newcastle Regional Art Gallery** (*Laman St. Tel: (02) 4974 5100. www.ncc.nsw.gov.au. Open: Tue–Sun 10am–5pm. Free admission*). A new Regional Museum is due to open in 2009.

The **Newcastle Visitor Information Centre** is also worth stopping in at (*361 Hunter St, opposite the Civic Rail Station. Tel: (02) 4974 2999. www.visitnewcastle.com.au. Open: Mon–Fri 9am–5pm, Sat & Sun 10am–4.30pm*).

Port Stephens and Nelson Bay

217km (135 miles) north of Sydney, 57km (35 miles) north of Newcastle
Port Stephens is essentially a conglomerate of pleasant waterfront suburbs that fringe the natural harbour of Port Stephens, with the harbourside settlement of Nelson Bay its recognised capital. Though off the main northbound highway, the region is fast developing into a major tourism destination.

The hills of the **Tomaree National Park** guard the harbour entrance and along with several fine ocean beaches provide the natural aesthetics that play such a large part in the region's popularity. The views that reward the 30-minute, strenuous ascent of Tomaree Head, at the far west end of Shoal Bay, are truly memorable, particularly at sunset or sunrise.

Further south, **Stockton Beach** extends over 30km (19 miles) all the way down to Newcastle and is the venue for 4WD or quad bike adventures as well as horse trekking and fishing.

Several cruise companies also operate out of Nelson Bay, with dolphin- or whale-watching their main *raison d'être*.

The **Port Stephens Visitor Information Centre** offers full activity and accommodation listings (*Victoria Parade. Tel: (02) 4980 6900. www.portstephens.org.au. Open: 9am–5pm*).

Pelicans await the return of fishermen at Elizabeth Beach, Myall Lakes

Myall Lakes National Park

260km (160 miles) north of Sydney,
100km (62 miles) north of Newcastle
The park (locally called Great Lakes) is one of the state's most popular coastal parks. It consists of 21,367ha (52,800 acres) of ocean beaches, headlands, inland waterways, lakes and eucalyptus forest.

The main settlements fringing the park are Tea Gardens and Hawks Nest (which sit on the northwestern shores of Port Stephens) to the south, Bulahdelah (on the Pacific Highway to the west), and Forster and Tuncurry (on the coast to the north). Within the park itself the small beachside villages of Seal Rocks and **Bluey's Beach** are excellent surf spots and throughout the park there are campsites with a good range of facilities.

The best way to explore the park fully is from south (via Hawks Nest) to north (Forster). The roads are unsealed but perfectly negotiable without 4WD. The *Great Lakes District Map*, available from local visitor centres, is an essential piece of kit for any visit.

If you are short of time, a trip to **Seal Rocks** is recommended. Follow the signposts off Lakes Way between Myall Lake and Smiths Lake, then head down Seal Rocks Rd (unsealed for 11km/7 miles) southwest to reach the coast and the pretty beachside settlement. Other than the superb surf beaches on both sides of the headland, the 2km (1¼-mile) walk to the Sugarloaf Point Lighthouse, past the Seal Rocks Blow Hole, is the main attraction.

The principal **Visitor Information Centre** is in Bulahdelah (*Corner of Pacific Highway & Crawford St. Tel: (02) 4997 4981 & 1800 802 692. www.greatlakes.org.au. Open: 9am–*

4pm). There are also smaller centres in Hawks Nest (*209 Myall St. Tel: (02) 4997 0749*) and Bluey's Beach (*Boomerang Dr. Tel: (02) 6554 0123*).

Forster and Tuncurry

300km (185 miles) north of Sydney
The twin coastal towns of Forster and Tuncurry have been a favourite domestic holiday destination for many years and form the northern gateway to the Great Lakes region. Although they possess some great beaches in their own right, thanks to the proximity to the delights of the Great Lakes region, the towns are mainly used as a convenient base for accommodation and essential services. **One Mile Beach** at the western fringe of Forster offers great views and good surfing, while just south of town is the northern fringe of the **Booti Booti National Park**. In essence, this comprises a narrow strip of land between Lake Wallis and the ocean, but this is only obvious from higher ground. For the best views, head to the lookout tower (40-minute return walk) at **Cape Hawke** (head east along Minor Rd off the Lakes Way). From the top you can see for miles, south along the coast towards Myall Lakes National Park, inland across Lake Wallis, and down to the small but hopelessly inviting **McBride's Beach**. McBride's is as good as it looks and the ideal place to escape for the day, provided you have the time and are up for the 20-minute walk from the parking area just west of the lookout car park.

The **Great Lakes Visitor Information Centre** is a good initial port of call (*beside the river on Little St, Forster. Tel: (02) 6554 8799 & 1800 802 692. www.greatlakes.org.au. Open: 9am–5pm*).

The New South Wales north coast

The view to Tuncurry over the beach

The wine and vineyards of the Hunter Valley

Along with the Yarra Valley in Victoria and the Barossa in South Australia, the Hunter Valley in New South Wales is synonymous with fine wines and conjures up the classic images of rolling hills at dawn, networked with rows of grape-laden vines. When it comes to pleasant rural aesthetics the Hunter certainly doesn't disappoint, but it has not always been so idyllic. With the discovery of coal in the late 1700s the region was rapidly transformed into one of the most industrialised in the country, earning it considerable wealth and bestowing upon it some very recognisable British place names, including Newcastle and Swansea. The Hunter River itself was originally called Coal River before being renamed in 1797 in honour of the then governor of the state.

Like any precious resource, however, it was exhaustible and over the decades there has been a steady transformation of both working practices and aesthetics, and although coal is still mined in the Hunter, you would hardly know it.

Scotsman James Busby planted the first vines as a non-commercial venture in the 1830s. His careful nurturing mixed with the favourable climate and soil did the rest and, with a vineyard boom in the 1970s and 80s, together with the highly successful promotion of the Hunter Valley as a prime tourism destination ever since, the area is now firmly on the international cork-poppers' map.

There are now over 160 vineyards in the region (90 with cellar doors where wine can be tasted and bought), the vast majority located in the Lower Hunter Valley and scattered around the small towns of Maitland, Singleton and Cessnock. The

Barrels of wine in a Hunter Valley winery

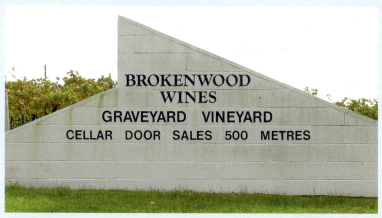

The entrance to one of the Brokenwood Wines vineyards, near Cessnock

remainder are located in the Upper Hunter Valley around Denman and Muswellbrook.

The Hunter is best known for its Shiraz, Sémillons and Chardonnays, and more recently for Merlot and Pinot Noir. But whatever the vintage the emphasis here is firmly focused on quality rather than quantity. The vineyards range from large-scale producers and internationally recognised labels like Lindemans and McGuigans to low-key boutique wineries like Pepper Tree and Oakvale. Some, like Draytons and Tullochs (at Pokolbin), are over a century old, while others are still staring past the barrels at saplings.

As you might expect, the great vineyard milieu is enhanced with numerous quality B&Bs, restaurants, art galleries and the inevitable adjunct attractions like boutique chocolate and cheese factories. Almost all are open year round and are especially busy at harvest time (Feb–Mar) and in the autumn. There is a vast array of tasting tour options and modes of transport on offer, from pedal power to horse-drawn carriages, or you can view it all from above by balloon.

The **Hunter Valley (Wine Country Tourism) Visitor Information Centre** is the principal visitor centre supplying detailed vineyard information as well as accommodation and tour bookings. It also has a café and winemaking display.
Hunter Valley Visitor Information Centre. 455 Wine Country Drive (4km/2½ miles north of Cessnock). Tel: (02) 4990 0900. www.winecountry.com.au. Open: Mon–Thur 9am–5.30pm, Fri 9am–6pm, Sat 9am–5pm, Sun 9am–4pm.

Port Macquarie

396km (246 miles) north of Sydney

One of the state's oldest settlements, Port Macquarie was first established as a penal colony in 1821. It is often overlooked by international tourists in their haste to get to Byron Bay, but remains a very popular domestic holiday destination and is certainly worthy of investigation, being only a short detour off the Pacific Highway.

The beaches that fringe the eastern suburbs are superb, offering excellent swimming, fishing, surfing and short walks.

Pockets of coastal native bush have survived intact and the region is well known for its resident koala population. Two interesting attractions showcase this natural asset. The 72ha (178-acre) coastal **Sea Acres Nature** is a preserved piece of rainforest and one of the best places in town to spot wild koala, particularly in the late afternoon (*Pacific Drive. Tel: (02) 6582 3355. Open: 9am–4.30pm. Admission charge, children under 7 free*). A short boardwalk meanders through the bush and finishes at the Rainforest Centre, which in itself houses an interesting range of displays, café and shop. Guided tours are available. The **Koala Hospital** in the Macquarie Nature Reserve displays some permanent and

The view looking south from Smoky Cape, South West Rocks

pre-release animals (*Lord St. Tel: (02) 6584 1522. Open: daily. Admission by donation*). Feeding takes place daily at 8am and 3pm. Another alternative is the **Billabong Koala Breeding Centre** 10km (6 miles) west of the town centre (*61 Billabong Dr, off Pacific Highway. Tel: (02) 6585 1060. Open: 9am–5pm. Admission charge*). It also has other native species on display.

There are also a number of interesting historical attractions in the town worth seeing, with the convict-built **Historical Museum** being the best place to start (*22 Clarence St. Tel: (02) 6583 1108. Open: Mon–Sat 9.30am–4.30pm. Admission charge*).

The **Visitor Information Centre** is located right in the heart of town (*Corner of Gordon St & Gore St. Tel: 1300 303 155. www.portmacquarieinfo.com.au. Open: Mon–Fri 8.30am–5pm, Sat & Sun 9am–4pm*).

South West Rocks

480km (300 miles) north of Sydney, 84km (52 miles) north of Port Macquarie South West Rocks used to be a well-kept secret but is now one of the fastest-developing holiday towns on the East Coast. Its long swathes of golden sand and the nearby **Hat Head National Park** are its major attractions.

At the eastern end of Trial Bay beach within the Arakoon State Recreation Area are the remains of the **Trial Bay Gaol**, built in 1886. It now houses a small museum that offers some

Looking north to Laurietown and towards Port Macquarie

sympathetic insight into the torrid existence of its former inmates (*Tel: (02) 6566 6168. Open: 9am–5pm. Admission charge*).

Nearby and at the northern end of the Hat Head National Park is the 1891 **Smoky Cape Lighthouse**, one of the tallest and oldest in NSW. The headland provides stunning views south to Crescent Head and north down to North Smoky Beach, which is accessible by a marked track. Another fine and more accessible alternative is Gap Beach, at the western end of Arakoon.

The main **Visitor Information Centre** is the Kempsey VIC (*South Kempsey Park, off Pacific Highway, Kempsey. Tel: 1800 642 480. www.kempsey.midcoast.com.au*).

Drive: Inland to Bellingen, Dorrigo and New England National Park

This drive offers a fine break from the coast, and the opportunity to explore cooler climes and the green rainforests of two of the state's finest national parks: Dorrigo and New England.

Allow a whole day for this 195km (121-mile) drive.

From Urunga on the Pacific Highway, go west on SH78 to Bellingen. Check out the **Visitor Information Centre** *(Pacific Highway, Urunga. Tel: (02) 6655 5711. www.bellingen.com. Open: Mon–Sat 9am–5pm, Sun 10am–2pm).*

1 Bellingen

160km (100 miles) from Port Macquarie Bellingen (known locally as 'Bello') is a charming village that sits on the banks of its namesake river and is renowned for its artistic and alternative

The view from Point Lookout, New England National Park

community, craft outlets, markets and – believe it or not – a bat colony!

Good craft outlets include the **Old Butter Factory** (*Doepel Lane*) and the unmistakable **Yellow Shed** (*Hyde St*). The colourful Bellingen craft and produce market is one of the best in the region and is held in the local park on the third Saturday of the month.

Even if you have an aversion to bats, that prejudice can be challenged with a stroll to the large fruit bat (flying fox) colony beside the river. The best place to view them is from the Bellingen Caravan Park on Dowle St, where you can observe them en masse around dusk when they depart to find food.
From Bellingen head west on SH78, climbing steeply to the Dorrigo Plateau and the National Parks and Wildlife Service (NPWS) Dorrigo National Park Rainforest Visitor Centre (signposted) just before the village of Dorrigo.

2 Dorrigo National Park

20km (12½ miles) from Bellingen
For many foreigners Dorrigo offers a first taste of Australian rainforest and the sheer density of the lush habitat

often comes as a surprise. The rainforest has a rich biodiversity with a plethora of everything from frogs to frogmouths (a species of bird).
Continue west to the village of Dorrigo.

3 Dorrigo village

30km (18½ miles) from Bellingen
The village of Dorrigo is almost entirely surrounded by national park and is the perfect place for refreshment. A visit to the **National Parks and Wildlife Service Rainforest Visitors Centre** (*Dome Rd, Dorrigo. Tel: (02) 6657 2309. www.nationalparks.nsw.gov.au*) gives a fine introduction to the area, with its 100m (330ft) skywalk above the rainforest canopy. There are some excellent rainforest walks that begin from the centre. Just north of Dorrigo (1.5km/1 mile), the Dangar Falls are worth a look, particularly after heavy rain when they become a thunderous torrent.
From Dorrigo continue west on SH78 (Waterfall Way) towards Armidale. About 10km (6 miles) past Ebor turn left in to the New England National Park along Point Lookout Rd.

4 New England National Park

The escarpments that make up this vast 67,303ha (166,300-acre) park form part of the Great Dividing Range and, provided the weather is clear, a visit to Point Lookout is worthwhile. Apart from the stunning views, there are also some excellent short walks that descend from the car park into the bush itself.

Coffs Harbour

572km (355 miles) north of Sydney
Conveniently located roughly halfway between Sydney and Brisbane, Coffs Harbour is a favourite domestic holiday resort and stopping point for those heading northward. Surrounded by rolling hills and host to some pretty beaches, it's a fine spot to kick back for a couple of days.

It is perhaps a sad reflection on modern marketing or human nature (or indeed both) that the one thing Coffs Harbour is most famous for is a 4m-long (13ft) bright yellow plastic banana, but for many years this has indeed been the case (*see p87*). Said banana is the moniker of the recently developed **Big Banana Complex**, one of the city's principal tourist attractions and a rather kitschy showcase for the region's principal agricultural export. It is located just north of the town and fronts a working banana plantation. There you can learn almost all you need to know about the favourite fruit, and enjoy a number of other long-established activities, such as toboggan rides, 'snow-tubing' and ice skating (*Tel: (02) 6652 4355. www.bigbanana.com. Open: 9am–4pm. Admission charge*).

Other than securing the obligatory photo with the big banana, activities are centred around the attractive marina where regular fishing, whale- and dolphin-watching cruises are on offer, together with highly popular diving

Coffs Harbour marina, as seen from Muttonbird Island

The Botanical Gardens at Coffs Harbour

and snorkelling trips to the outlying **Solitary Islands Marine Reserve**. The whale-watching season runs from June to September.

Linked to the mainland by the marina's sea wall is **Muttonbird Island Nature Reserve**, an important breeding ground for wedge-tailed shearwaters. These ocean wanderers breed from October to April and nest in a warren of burrows across the entire island. They are best viewed just after dusk, when they return in large numbers to feed their young. Even out of season the headland offers a pleasant walk and good views back across the town.

Other good local attractions include the **Botanical Gardens** (*Hardacre St. Tel: (02) 6648 4188. Open: 9am–5pm. Free admission*).

More information is available at the **Visitor Information Centre** (*Corner of Elizabeth St & Maclean St. Tel: (02) 6648 4990. www.coffscoast.com. au. Open: 9am–5pm*).

THE WOLLEMI PINE

With a landscape so vast and so ancient, it is little wonder that new plant and animal species are still being discovered in Australia. One of the most remarkable in recent years is the Wollemi pine (*Wollemia nobilis*), a species thought to have become extinct about 30 million years ago. It was discovered by a park ranger deep in the almost impenetrable limestone gorges and escarpments of the vast 493,594ha (1,219,692-acre) Wollemi National Park in New South Wales. But what makes this discovery particularly remarkable is the fact that it is only 129km (80 miles) northwest of Sydney, a modern city of 4 million people.

North to Byron Bay
Yamba and Iluka

169km (105 miles) north of Coffs Harbour
The small coastal fishing towns of Yamba and Iluka that sit on either side of the Clarence River mouth, and 13km (8 miles) east of the Pacific Highway, both offer a pleasant diversion from the mainstream tourist destinations along the north NSW coast. Both have some excellent surf beaches and of the two, Yamba is the larger and has better facilities. Like two green bookends the national parks of **Yuragyir** and **Bundjalung** lie south of Yamba and north of Iluka respectively,

and are also worth exploring on foot or by 4WD (vehicle permit purchasable at park entrances). There are also some fine and more accessible short walks, with the 2.5km (1½-mile) World Heritage Rainforest walk through the 136ha (336-acre) **Iluka Nature Reserve**

The unspoilt coastline at Lennox Head

Surf club competition at Byron Bay

River Bridge. Tel: (02) 6645 4121. www.clarencetourism.com. Open: 9am–5pm).

Lennox Head

20km (12½ miles) south of Byron Bay
The small, beachside settlement of Lennox Head is famous for its surf breaks and, either with or without a board, offers a quiet alternative destination to the commercial tourism chaos of Byron Bay only 15 minutes north. The heads themselves offer some fine views up towards Cape Byron and are a prime site for hang-gliding and dolphin-spotting. In season (June to November) you may also be lucky enough to see migrating whales. At the northern end of the village Lake Ainsworth is a fine locale for freshwater swimming, canoeing and windsurfing. The lake edge also serves as the venue for the local markets that are held on the second and fifth Sundays of each month.

being the most notable. The Clarence River Delta and **Lake Wooloweyah** (4km/2½ miles south of Yamba) also provide a wealth of boating, fishing and cruising opportunities.

The Yamba-Iluka ferry shuttles back and forth daily, so you can base yourself in either location. If you are camping, the Queensland Parks and Wildlife Service (QPWS) **Woody Head Campsite** near Iluka has to be one of the best coastal campsites in the state.

For more information and details, the **Clarence Coast Visitor Information Centre** should be your port of call
~rry Park, just off the Pacific Highway, 5km/3 miles south of the Clarence

NEW SOUTH WALES DRIVING TIMES

Sydney to Katoomba	122km (76 miles)
	3 hours
Sydney to Newcastle	167km (104 miles)
	3 hours
Newcastle to	253km (157 miles)
Port Macquarie	4½ hours
Port Macquarie to	159km (99 miles)
Coffs Harbour	2½ hours
Coffs Harbour to	237km (147 miles)
Byron Bay	4 hours
Byron Bay to	100km (62 miles)
Surfers Paradise	1½ hours

Byron Bay becomes a riot of colour and activity durig the summer

Byron Bay

800km (500 miles) north of Sydney

As little as 30 years ago, Byron Bay was just another sleepy coastal enclave, home to laid-back surfers and artists. Today, it is one of the 'hottest' tourist destinations in the state and some say it is in danger of boiling over altogether. It has gone from fairly busy to utterly manic and property prices are now something that would make an artist weep in disbelief.

That said, Byron remains alluring and hopelessly attractive, and seldom disappoints. Perhaps it is a mix of its alternative roots, or its lack of conformity. Here, drive-in fast-food outlets and multi-storey buildings have been banned from even attempting to swagger into town. Maybe it is the cosmopolitan nature of the place, the mix of well-to-do with transient backpacker. Or perhaps it's simply the beautiful surroundings... somehow it all gels into something irresistible.

When it comes to natural attractions, 37km (23 miles) of beaches, some of which offer world-class surfing conditions, are an obvious draw and not surprisingly there is even a naturist beach. Crowned by an almost iconic and much-photographed lighthouse, **Cape Byron** is the most easterly point in Australia. Dolphins often make an appearance alongside surfers here, if only to play games and make it all look oh-so-simple beneath the clumsy boards. Humpback whales are also a regular sight during their annual migrations in mid-winter and early summer.

Back in town, retail therapy is very well accommodated, with everything from polka-dot bikinis to new-age lava lamps. Alternative and health therapies are also big business, as attested by numerous boutique spas.

Byron Bay also has a wealth of activity operators offering everything from surf lessons and bike hire to skydiving and kayaking. One of the most popular pursuits is a guided dive trip to the nearby Julian Rocks Marine Park, rated as one of the top ten scuba diving locations in Australia.

The **Visitor Information Centre** has full activity and accommodation listings (*80 Jonston St. Tel: (02) 6680 8558. www.visitbyronbay.com. Open: 9am–5pm*).

Byron Bay hinterland

Inland from Byron Bay, the so-called Rainbow Region is an area rich with national parks and bohemian, arty villages. Dominating the skyline is the eroded volcanic vent of the World Heritage-listed **Mount Warning**. In essence, the entire region is a vast caldera (crater), stretching almost 60km (37 miles) inland and one of the largest of its type in the southern hemisphere. Nine national parks in the area offer magnificent scenery and walking opportunities, with Mount Warning National Park one of the most popular and accessible. The 1,157m (3,795ft) summit of Mount Warning is itself the target for many, especially at dawn. A number of tour operators in Byron Bay offer guided trips and transportation.

For detailed information call or visit the **World Heritage Rainforest**
Centre (*Corner of Tweed Valley Way & Alma St, Murwillumbah. Tel: (02) 6672 1340. www.tweedtourism.com.au. Open: 9am–4pm*).

To the south of Mount Warning is the once sleepy dairy village of **Nimbin**, which, ever since the infamous and inaugural Aquarius Festival of 1973, has steadily morphed into the undisputed Australian capital of 'the experimental and the alternative'. The colourful main street (and its equally colourful residents) is arguably the single collective 'sight' in the village. Amid laid-back cafés, alternative health and arts and craft shops (not to mention the odd wisp of smoke), the **Nimbin Museum** (*62 Cullen St. Tel: (02) 6689 1123. Open: 9am–5pm. Admission charge*) goes some way to explaining the village's intriguing history and alternative vision.

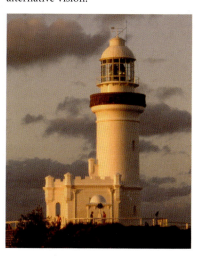

Cape Byron lighthouse sits at the easternmost point on mainland Australia

The Gold Coast

Gold Coast Australia. Even the words are, to the imagination, like lighting the blue touch paper and standing well back. Long golden beaches backed by high-rise apartments; fit, bronzed bodies baking in the sun; surfers riding the waves; smart retirees dripping with 'bling'; bustling shopping malls; boom boom nightclubs... Australia's answer to Miami and the Spanish Costas hosts over half a million visitors a year and is everything you might expect – and precious little else.

For lovers of the beach lifestyle, socialites, shopoholics and the press-button-wow-what's-next junkies, this is indeed the perfect happy storm and a wallet's worst nightmare. But what about those whose eyes roll heavenward at the sight of a mere roadsign to the place? Take the city by-pass? Head for the hills? Well, actually no. Believe it or not, you should go anyway. The chances are, amid all the derision of excess and the superficiality, you will actually have a blast. Yes, folks, it is time. Time to throw off the serious shackles of sophistication, put on your best (and tightest) swimming cossie, buy a Big Mac whopperoo and head for the beach.

Stretching for almost 45km (28 miles) from Coolangatta in the south to Nerang Head in the north, the Gold Coast is, in essence, one long sweep of azure water with regulation surf, breaking tirelessly upon golden beach backed by a towering forest of glistening apartment blocks. Again, just as you might imagine. There is very little distinction between the major centres along the coast, bar perhaps the number and height of the apartment blocks that reach a lofty crescendo at Surfers Paradise. 'Surfers' is the epicentre of all the action, where the shopping malls, apartments blocks, backpacker hostels, clubs and restaurants converge into one mass 24-hour yahoo.

The Gold Coast is also home to a number of high-profile action-packed theme parks, including Sea World, Movie World, and Wet 'n' Wild (*see p165*). Although expensive, they rarely prove a disappointment and are a dream come true for children. Other activities abound here, too, with everything on offer from fishing to skydiving.

Then, should it all get a bit much, or your wallet holds nought but a few grains of sand, then you can always find sanctuary in the 'green behind the gold' in the form of the Springbrook and Lamington National Parks, two of Queensland's best.

COOLANGATTA TO SURFERS PARADISE

Coolangatta

104km (65 miles) south of Brisbane, 25km (15½ miles) south of Surfers Paradise.

Strategically positioned next to the Tweed River mouth and right on the border of New South Wales and Queensland, Coolangatta was one of the earliest settlements on the Gold Coast, established in the 1860s, and is the surfing centre of this coast. The formation of the beaches and rock platforms surrounding Point Danger create excellent surf breaks that have a reputation as some of the best and most consistent in the world.

Not surprisingly then, it is all beach and surfing here. The main beaches are patrolled in summer and so are safe for children, and the town has a wide range

The Gold Coast

of facilities. The best place to watch the surfing action is from Snapper Rocks at the end of Rainbow Bay.

Currumbin

17km (10¹/₂ miles) south of Surfers Paradise

The big attraction here is the **Currumbin Wildlife Sanctuary**, one of the most popular wild animal parks on the East Coast. It houses all the usual suspects, from Tasmanian Devils to crocodiles, but the highlight is the wild rainbow lorikeet feeding. Described as an 'avian-human interaction spectacular' it is a truly memorable experience and involves feeding these screeching, almost impossibly colourful birds en masse. Given that much of Australia's native wildlife is nocturnal, they also offer a recommended 'Wildnight' tour (*7.20–9.45pm*), which includes an Aboriginal dance display.

Just off the Gold Coast Highway, Currumbin. Tel (07) 5534 1266. www.currumbin-sanctuary.org.au. Open: 8am–5pm, lorikeet feeding 8am & 4pm. Admission charge.

Burleigh Heads

8km (5 miles) south of Surfers Paradise

The remnants of an ancient volcano, Burleigh Heads forms one of the few breaks in the seemingly endless swathe

Greenmount Beach from Pat Fagan Park, Coolangatta

of golden sand and offers some world-class surf breaks and several good walking tracks through the **Burleigh Head National Park** (*Tel: (07) 5535 3032. www.epa.qld.gov.au*). There are also some beachfront restaurants with memorable views up to Surfers.

Surfers Paradise

It seems hard to imagine that as little as 50 years ago, all that really caught the eye here was the surf, the sand and a few holiday homes including the Surfers Paradise Hotel. Yet, like some proliferate commercial weed, it has grown into the vast conglomerate of commercialism and property development we see today.

Amid the apartment blocks, one high-rise known as **Q1** stands out above the rest. You can take in the views from the 77th-floor observation deck of this 'world's highest residential building', or indulge yourself at its in-house spa or cocktail bar (*Tel: 1300 792 008. www.Q1.com.au. Open: Fri & Sat 9am–midnight, Sun–Thur 9am–9pm. Admission charge*).

Given all the kitsch on display, a fine alternative is the **Gold Coast City Art Centre** (*135 Bundall Rd. Tel (07) 5581 6500. www.gcac.com.au. Open: Mon–Fri 10am–5pm, Sat & Sun 11am–5pm. Free admission*). It offers a dynamic programme of local contemporary work as well as visiting exhibitions and a wide-ranging historical collection. The outdoor sculpture walk is also worth doing.

Admiring the view from the beach at Coolangatta

North of Surfers, **Main Beach** fringes the southern shores of Broadwater Bay and the Nerang River Inlet. The **Marina Mirage** shopping complex is the main attraction here, containing some of the best restaurants in the region. It is also the departure point for most scenic cruises and helicopter flights and the location of the impressive 5-star Palazzo Versace Hotel. North of Main Beach is the coast's most impressive theme park, **Sea World** (*see p69*).

Pop into the **Visitor Information Centre** for more information (*Cavill Ave Mall, Surfers Paradise. Tel (07) 5538 4419. www.goldcoasttourism.com.au. Open: Mon–Fri 8.30am–5.30pm, Sat 8.30am–5pm, Sun 9am–4pm*).

Gold Coast theme parks

Almost by default, the Gold Coast has become Australia's theme park capital, with the high-profile stalwarts Sea World, Movie World and Wet 'n' Wild between them attracting millions of visitors annually. Adrenaline junkies can swim with sharks, or go from 0 to 100kph (62mph) in just 2 seconds aboard the Superman Escape, while the kids can meet Shrek, kiss Tweety Pie and pat Bugs Bunny.

At A$66 for adults and A$43 for children one-off entry is hardly cheap, but that usually includes most rides and attractions, which provides a very full day of entertainment. There is also a Super Pass allowing unlimited entry for 14 days to all the major parks for A$177 (children A$115) and The Fun Pass allowing one single day's entry to each park for A$142 (children A$89).

Visitor information centres can help you secure the latest discounts, or you can book online (*www.myfun.com.au*).

Movie World

Due to the marketing power of Hollywood these days, Movie World is perhaps the most popular of all the theme parks on the Gold Coast and attracts children like bees to honey.

But it is not all about the kids. Like its competitors, it offers a wide mix of state-of-the-art attractions for both young and old, from thrill rides to stunt shows. Of course there is plenty to keep the kids occupied, and all the usual suspects are in evidence to meet and greet, including Batman, Scooby Doo and Shrek. Overall, it makes for a highly entertaining and stimulating mix of sights, sounds and action that requires at least one full day.
Pacific Highway, Oxenford.
Tel: (07) 5573 8485.
www.myfun.com.au. Open: 10am–5.30pm. Admission charge.

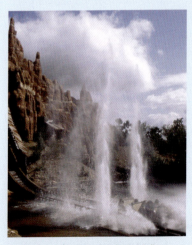

Making a splash on the Wild West Falls Adventure Ride at the Gold Coast's Movie World

On a hot day, aptly named Wet 'n' Wild Water World offers the perfect relief

Sea World

Sea World enjoys a reputation as one of the world's best theme parks, offering a wide array of cutting-edge marine-based attractions including dolphin and seal shows, thrill rides and water-ski stunts, polar bear Kanook and Ping Ping and, the most recent addition, a multi-million-dollar shark exhibit. In tune with most East Coast wildlife parks, interaction plays an important role and at Sea World you can (for a fee) get in the water with dolphins or seals, be a trainer for a day, or even get up close and personal with the sharks. Then, of course, should all that seem far too tame, you can always go and hang out with Big Bird or the Cookie Monster at Sesame Street Beach.

Main Beach. Tel: (07) 5588 2205.
www.myfun.com.au.
Open: 10am–5pm. Admission charge.

Wet 'n' Wild Water World

As the name suggests, here it's man meets water in just about every conceivable way. There are rides and slides from the gentle to the jaw-dropping, wave machines, dive-in movies… and it all comes complete with the inevitable aqua staff and splash cash. Wet and wild it certainly is and on a hot Gold Coast day there is no doubting this is the place to be.

Pacific Highway, Oxenford.
Tel: (07) 5573 8485.
www.myfun.com.au.
Open: 10am–5pm. Admission charge.

Springbrook, Lamington and Mount Tamborine National Parks

Less than an hour's drive from Surfers Paradise is true paradise. Dubbed 'the Green behind the Gold', the national parks of Springbrook, Lamington and Mount Tamborine collectively offer a natural wonder-world of pristine subtropical rainforest, waterfalls, walking tracks and stunning views, and are the perfect escape from the heat and hype of the coast.

There are **QPWS offices** (Queensland Parks and Wildlife Service) located within the first two parks, and a **Visitor Information Centre** in Mount Tamborine. Walking track guides with maps and details are available from each office: *Springbrook. Tel: (07) 5533 5147. www.epa.qld.gov.au Lamington. Tel: (07) 5544 0634. www.epa.qld.gov.au Mount Tamborine Visitor Information Centre. Doughty Park, off Main Western Rd, North Tamborine. Tel (07) 5545 3200. www.tamborinetourism.com.au*

Springbrook National Park

The 2,954ha (7,300-acre) Springbrook National Park is the most accessible to the coast and sits on the northern rim of the vast Mount Warning (Scenic Rim) volcanic caldera. The park is spilt into three sections: Springbrook Plateau, Natural Bridge and the Cougals. Combined, they offer a rich subtropical rainforest habitat of ancient trees and gorges, interspersed with creeks, waterfalls and an extensive system of walking tracks. In addition, the park is well known for its rich biodiversity and spectacular views. Other attractions include the Natural Arch, a cavernous rock archway that spans Cave Creek. *31km (19½ miles) southwest of Surfers Paradise.*

A baby skink takes shelter under a leaf

The Tawny Frogmouth is just one of Lamington's many avian residents

Lamington National Park

The 20,500ha (50,660-acre) Lamington National Park is about 60km (37 miles) inland from the Gold Coast and, like Springbrook, it offers a wealth of superb natural features and a rich biodiversity that is best experienced by exploring an extensive network of walking tracks. The park is essentially split into two sections: the Binna Burra to the east and the Green Mountains to the west. The park also plays host to two famous and long-established guesthouses: O'Reilly's and Binna Burra. For many, a short stay here offers the perfect (and comfortable) introduction to the intriguing rainforest environment and many of its most exotic wild inhabitants, including that great avian mimic, the lyrebird.

60km (37 miles) southwest of Surfers Paradise.

Mount Tamborine and surrounds

The Mount Tamborine region encompasses the Tamborine National Park and the picturesque settlements of Mount Tamborine, Tamborine Village and Eagle Heights. Together they offer fine coastal views, pleasant walking tracks, vineyards, B&Bs, art galleries and craft outlets. The most popular areas of the park are the Cedar Creek and Witches Falls sections, which feature some pretty waterfalls and short walks.

47km (29 miles) west of Surfers Paradise.

QUEENSLAND DRIVING TIMES

Surfers Paradise to Brisbane	78km (48 miles) 1½ hours	
Brisbane to Noosa Heads	145km (90 miles) 2½ hours	
Noosa Heads to Hervey Bay	187km (116 miles) 3½ hours	
Hervey Bay to Bundaberg	125km (78 miles) 2 hours	
Bundaberg to Rockhampton	319km (198 miles) 4 hours	
Rockhampton to Mackay	348km (216 miles) 4 hours	
Mackay to Airlie Beach	160km (100 miles) 2½ hours	
Airlie Beach to Townsville	303km (188 miles) 4½ hours	
Townsville to Cairns	361km (224 miles) 5½ hours	

Brisbane

With Aboriginal tribes having frequented the region for over 40,000 years, the first substantial European explorations of the Brisbane region were made in 1823 by the explorer John Oxley. His mission was to find a suitable site for a new penal colony intended to take the worst convicts from the fast-developing free settlement of Sydney, 970km (600 miles) to the south. After a failed attempt on the coast, the settlement was finally established up the river (christened 'The Brisbane') at North Quay.

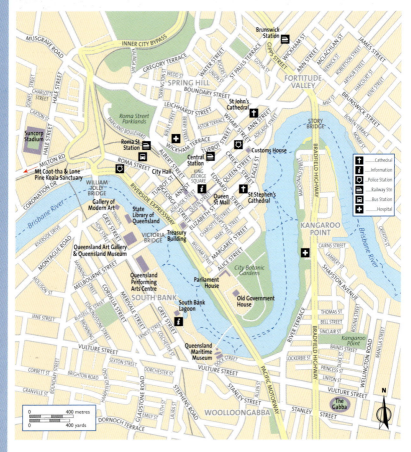

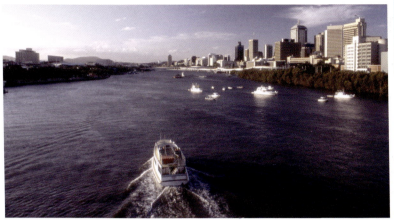

Brisbane city centre viewed from the Goodwill Bridge

The new and initially notorious penal colony soon developed into an established free settlement that grew from strength to strength and ultimately into the glistening tropical high-rise forest we see today.

With such strong competition from Sydney, Melbourne and Perth, Brisbane was for many years seen as the nation's poor cousin and labelled as backward and non-progressive. However, Queenslanders (and more especially the good people of Brisbane) would have none of it, and after hosting some internationally important events like the Commonwealth Games in 1982, Expo 88 and, most recently, the 2001 Goodwill Games, the city enjoyed phenomenal growth and now stands independent and proud upon the world's urban scene.

Brisbane enjoys an almost perfect climate, which plays a key role in attracting over 5 million visitors annually and permeates almost every aspect of city life. Al fresco restaurants, cafés and outdoor attractions dominate, and the Brisbane River is a major feature and is also very important for transport. The city's greatest tourist attraction is South Bank, the former site of Expo 88. It is here in the shadow of the CBD (Central Business District) that most of the major cultural venues are based. South Bank also features its very own inner-city swimming lagoon and beach, which for visitors from colder climes often proves to be the most memorable aspect of their stay.

Away from the city centre, other notable attractions are the Lone Pine Koala Sanctuary and Mt Coot-tha, offering impressive views across the city.

Brisbane also serves as the gateway to the Moreton Bay Islands, some of the most beautiful and unspoiled on the Queensland Coast.

Brisbane's iconic Story Bridge

The city centre

Brisbane's Central Business District is built around the gentle meanderings of the Brisbane River, which in itself provides a convenient way to get from A to B. Being effectively bounded by water on all but its northerly edge, the CBD is relatively compact, with streets laid out in a simple grid system. Most activity centres around the shopping malls and precincts of Queen St and Adelaide St.

The **Visitor Information Centre** offers free city maps and more (*Queen St Mall, between Albert & Edward Streets. Tel: (07) 3006 6290. www.experiencebrisbanetourism.com. Open: Mon–Thur 9am–5.30pm, Fri 9am–7pm, Sat 9am–5pm, Sun 9.30am–4.30pm*).

Historical buildings

Amid the growing stand of high-rises there are some historical buildings worthy of investigation. At the top end of Albert St facing King George Square is the **City Hall** with its Italian Renaissance-style clock tower. Built in 1930, it was dubbed the 'Million-Pound Town Hall', which was a controversially extravagant amount that would now scarcely raise an eyebrow at the auction of a high-end inner-city apartment. You can access the top of the tower via a lift (*Open: Mon–Fri 10am–3pm. Free admission*). Housed in City Hall is the **Brisbane Museum**, showcasing the capital's social history, visual arts, craft and design (*Tel: (07) 3403 8888. Open: 8am–5pm. Admission charge, guided tours available*).

On George St alongside the riverbank is the grand 19th-century façade of the former **Treasury Building**. Although still dealing with money matters, it does so in a far more casual and transitory nature as the city's casino (*Tel: (07) 3306 8888. Open: 24 hours*).

To the west beside the Botanic Gardens is the 1868 French Renaissance-style **Parliament House**, commissioned when Queensland was declared a separate colony in 1859 (*Tel: (07) 3406 7111. Open: Mon–Fri 9am–5pm*). Free tours are available (*Mon–Fri five times daily*) and you can also watch proceedings. Nearby, the 1862 **Old Government House** is currently being refurbished and will reopen to the public in 2009.

Further north, like a miniature version of St Paul's Cathedral in London, is the 1889 **Customs House** (*399 Queen St. Tel: (07) 3365 8999*). It contains a small art gallery and café. Nearby are Brisbane's two main cathedrals: the 1901 Gothic-style **St John's Cathedral** (*Ann St*) and 1874 **St Stephen's Catholic Cathedral** (*Charlotte St*). Dominating the river west of the CBD is the iconic **Story Bridge**. Built between 1935 and 1940, it has some of the deepest foundations of any such structure in the world – 42m (138ft). The city is hoping to emulate the huge success of the Sydney Harbour Bridge Climb with its new **Story Bridge Adventure Climb** (*Tel: (07) 3514 6900. www.storybridgeadventureclimb.com.au. Admission charge*). Although a far cry from the Harbour Bridge, the secure 2½-hour climb offers fine views across the city from the 80m (262ft) span, particularly at dawn or dusk.

Parks and gardens

The city hosts some fine parks and formal gardens, the **Botanic Gardens** being the oldest (*Alice St. Tel: (07) 3403 2535*). East of the CBD is the more contemporary 16ha (40-acre) **Roma Street Parkland** (*1 Parkland Boulevard. Tel: (07) 3006 4545. www.romastreetparkland.qld.gov.au*). Dubbed the 'world's largest urban subtropical gardens', they host an impressive mix of open space, urban landscape design and contemporary art installations, plus there's a licensed café.

The tower of Brisbane City Hall rises above a sculpture in King George Square

South Bank

South Bank is the former site of Expo 88. Taking up around 17ha (42 acres), it is home to almost all of the city's major cultural establishments. Surrounding them is an impressive contemporary outdoor recreation space, the centrepiece of which is the hugely popular South Bank Lagoon, complete with inner-city beach.

South Bank is easily accessed by foot from the CBD or via the river with City Cat ferry services.

There is a **Visitor Information Centre** located behind the lagoon complex (*Tel: (07) 3867 2051.*

www.visitsouthbank.com. Open: Mon–Thur & Sat 9am–6pm, Fri 9am–10pm).

Gallery of Modern Art (GoMA)

The GoMA is Australia's largest gallery, with a staggering 5,825sq m (62,700sq ft) of exhibition space on five levels. The gallery also boasts Australia's first Cinemateque, a state-of-the-art purpose-built facility to showcase the art of film.

Stanley Place. Tel: (07) 3840 7303. www.qag.qld.gov.au. Open: Mon–Fri 10am–5pm, Sat & Sun 9am–5pm. Free admission, tours available daily.

Brisbane's South Bank

Queensland Art Gallery (QAG)

The QAG is considered Brisbane's premier arts attraction, displaying an impressive collection of Aboriginal, European, Asian and contemporary Australian art. It also hosts major visiting or special exhibitions.
Melbourne St. Tel: (07) 3840 7303. www.qag.qld.gov.au. Open: Mon–Fri 10am–5pm, Sat & Sun 9am–5pm. Free admission, tours available daily.

Queensland Museum

Especially renowned for its prehistoric and natural history displays, this museum also hosts absorbing collections of indigenous and early European artefacts and places a heavy emphasis on the hands-on and interpretive approach.
Grey St. Tel: (07) 3840 7555. www.Qmuseum.qld.gov.au. Open: 9.30am–5pm. Free admission, except for special exhibitions.

Queensland Performing Arts Centre

This multifarious high-profile complex houses the Lyric Theatre, Concert Hall, Cremorne Theatre and Optus Playhouse, which in turn are home to the state's leading performing arts companies: the Queensland Theatre Company, Queensland Ballet, Queensland Orchestra and Opera Queensland. They offer an exciting and on-going programme of events. It also has a restaurant and café.
Melbourne St. Tel: (07) 3840 7444. www.qpac.com.au

A DAY AT THE RACES

One of the nation's most unusual events is the annual cockroach races held on Australia Day (26 Jan) at Brisbane's Story Bridge Hotel. The races, founded in 1980, now attract hundreds of spectators and – rumour has it – some fine thoroughbred roaches. Led proudly onto the racing floor by highland pipers, the insects are held in a bowl and then released. Amid wild excitement, the winner is the first speedster over the line of a 5m (16½ft) circle. After various heats, the winner's owner takes all, which is usually a lot of beer.

South Bank Lagoon

The outdoor South Bank Lagoon complex is a superb location to kick back and relax. The water is crystal clear, and the beach even cleaner (*Open: daily. Lifeguards on duty: Dec & Jan 7am–midnight, Feb & Mar 7am–7pm, Apr–Aug 9am–5pm, 1 Sept–20 Sept 9am–6pm, 21 Sept–30 Nov 7am–7pm. Free admission*).

Just behind the complex is the venue for the colourful **South Bank markets** (*Open: Fri night, Sat & Sun*) and the 'Al Fresco Cinema' (*Open: Wed–Sat (Feb–Mar)*).

State Library of Queensland

This is Australia's leading library for Queensland's document heritage, and it also features a unique Indigenous Knowledge Centre (IKC), the first of its kind in Australia. The impressive library also offers free internet access, but you must book (*Tel: (07) 3840 7810*).
Stanley Place. Tel: (07) 3840 7666. www.slq.qld.gov.au

City surrounds

Lone Pine Koala Sanctuary

Lone Pine is the world's oldest and largest depository of these enchanting, famously adorable, yet utterly pea-brained tree dwellers. Having opened in 1927 and now housing around 130, it offers a fine introduction and the obligatory cuddle and photo session. Also on display are other natives like wombats, echidnas and kangaroos. *Jesmond Rd, Fig Tree Pocket (southwest via Milton Rd and the western Freeway 5). Tel: (07) 3378 1366. www.koala.net.au. Open: 8am–5pm. Admission charge. Bus: 430 from the 'koala platform' in the Myer Centre, Queen St. Boat: Mirimar Boat Cruise departs daily from North Quay at 10am (Tel: (07) 3221 0300).*

Mt Coot-tha

The 52ha (128-acre) **Brisbane Botanic Gardens** (*Via Milton Rd, off Roma St. Tel: (07) 3403 8888. Open: 8.30am–5.30pm. Free admission*) at Mt Coot-tha are a renowned subtropical garden featuring over 20,000 specimens of 5,000 species. To show off the impressive inventory there are numerous specialist features, including a herbarium, tropical dome, bonsai house, and water-lily ponds. Within the grounds you will also find the **Lakeside Restaurant** (*Tel: (07) 3870 9506. Open: Mon–Sat 11.30am–2.30pm, Sun 8am–2.30pm*) and the botanically oriented **Miskin Art Gallery** (*Open: Tue–Sat 10am–4.30pm*). There are several short walks on offer, including an Aboriginal Plant Trail and an Australian

One of the koalas at the Lone Pine Koala Sanctuary

79

Brisbane

The Tropical Dome at the Botanic Gardens, Mount Coot-tha

Bus: 'City Sights' tour, or 471 from Adelaide St, stop 44, opposite City Hall (Tel: 131 230).

Mt Coot-tha Forest Park
Backing onto the Mt Coot-tha lookout complex is Mt Coot-tha Forest Park, which consists of 1,500ha (3,700 acres) of eucalypt forest, networked with walking tracks and containing over 350 native species. The park is just part of the vast 30,000ha (74,130-acre) expanse of the **Brisbane Forest Park** that backs onto the city, again boasting an astonishing range of wildlife, over 30km (19 miles) of walking tracks, and opportunities for horse trekking, mountain biking and bush camping. *Park headquarters & information centre. 'The Gap', Nebo Rd, west of the city centre. Tel: 1300 723 684. www.epa.qld.gov.au*

Plant Communities Trail, and guided tours of the gardens are available daily (*11am & 1pm*).

Set above the gardens and reached either by foot or car is the Mt Coot-tha Lookout, which offers expansive views across the city and out across Moreton Bay. The Summit Restaurant and Café (*see Directory listing p166*) provides an ideal venue for lunch, dinner or just a glass of wine while soaking up both the sun and the city vistas. The word 'Coot-tha' is Aboriginal in origin, meaning 'place of native honey'.

BUSH FIRES
Bush fires have always been a natural phenomenon in the Australian ecosystem and many native plants in particular rely on fire to reproduce. However, humankind's wholesale and unnatural alteration of habitat and land use in the last 200 years, together with the increasing effects of climate change, have dramatically increased the risk and severity of fires in recent decades. In 1994, 1996, 1997, 2001, 2002 and, most recently, 2006, fires ravaged national parks and the fringes of major towns and cities in almost all states, destroying numerous properties and taking several lives. Through their unpredictability and sheer ferocity they provide a powerful reminder of our impact on the environment and our fragile place within it.

Boat excursion: Tangalooma Dolphins and Moreton Bay Island

This excursion to the sand island of Moreton Bay offers a superb 'island experience' and the opportunity to feed wild dolphins at the world-famous Tangalooma Wild Dolphin Resort. The best way to reach the island is through the resort, which offers accommodation, day trips, a range of tours and independent transfers (see panel opposite). Pre-booking is required. See page 83 for map.

Allow a whole day.

The resort catamaran leaves from the terminal on the northern bank of the Brisbane River, at the end of Holt St, Pinkemba. To get there, from the city and western suburbs head along Kingsford Smith Drive, then approximately 2km (1¼ miles) past the Gateway Motorway overpass, turn right into Holt St and follow to the end. A resort coach operates from city hotels and the Roma St Transit Centre in Brisbane city centre (Bay 22, Level 3) at 7.30am, 10am, 12.30pm and 5pm (Tel: (07) 3637 2000 or 1300 652 250). The crossing takes 70 minutes.

1 Moreton Bay

From the Brisbane River mouth the huge expanse of Moreton Bay is sheltered from the ocean by over 300 low-lying sand islands deposited over the eons by ocean currents and stretching from Southport on the Gold Coast to Caloundra on the Sunshine Coast. The four largest are South and North Stradbroke Islands, Moreton Island and Bribie Island. Almost like an echo of their far more famous and visited relative Fraser Island further north, the beauty of the Moreton group lies in the fact that they are so easily accessible and remarkably unspoiled.

2 Moreton Island

Moreton Island is a national park in its own right and lies 37km (23 miles) northeast of the Brisbane River mouth.

Feeding wild dolphins at Tangalooma

Pelican feeding time on Moreton Island

With the exception of one high-profile resort, it is uninhabited and set aside for wilderness camping. Although not as large as Fraser Island, or host to nearly the same remarkable biodiversity, it does share a fine reputation for 4WD opportunities, shipwrecks and the ease with which you can escape to find complete solitude. Above all, Moreton is famous for its pod of friendly dolphins, which, with the lure of free feed, come every evening to the pier at the **Tangalooma Wild Dolphin Resort** to meet and greet an expectant crowd of resort guests and day-trippers.

There are around 600 to 800 Inshore Bottlenose dolphins within Moreton Bay itself and, of those, staff and researchers have individually identified around 127 at the resort. Around ten visit regularly, with names like Storm,

Fred and Karma and, as it is a wild pod, this regular interaction and observation have offered some great opportunities for research. There are a variety of other marine creatures that take advantage of the free feed, including rays, fish and squid. Warren, the Wobbegong shark (a non-aggressive species), also makes a regular appearance.

PRACTICALITIES

Tangalooma Wild Dolphin Resort
Offers full-day tours, dolphin-feeding and watching and an excellent range of island excursions and activities, from sand-boarding, snorkelling and diving to scenic helicopter flights. Daily whale-watching cruises are also available from June to October.
Tel: 1300 652 250 & (07) 3637 2118.
www.tangalooma.com
Dolphin Wild
Also offers day cruises to Moreton Island from Redcliffe, or from Brisbane for an extra charge.
Tel: (07) 3880 4444. www.dolphinwild.com.au

Sunshine and Fraser coasts

About an hour north of Brisbane, the intriguing scatter of volcanic peaks known as the Glass House Mountains herald your arrival in the Sunshine Coast region. Although the name might lack sophistication, with the area enjoying around 300 days of sunshine a year, it is at least an accurate description. The Sunshine Coast stretches around 45km (28 miles) from Bribie Island in Moreton Bay to Noosa Heads, and roughly the same distance inland to Nambour and the Blackall Range.

In the south are the popular, mainly domestic, holiday resorts of Mooloolaba and Maroochydore. Lacking the glitz and hype of the Gold Coast as well as its lofty swathe of apartment blocks, they present a quieter, less commercial holiday alternative.

Given the abiding constraints of time, however, the vast majority of international tourists head north, to the high-profile resort of Noosa Heads. Noosa is without doubt the most popular resort south of Cairns, boasting beautiful beaches, a national park, numerous activities and a wealth of attractive accommodation. It is also one of the most sought-after residential postal codes in Australia.

If you can manage to drag yourself away from the beach, the Sunshine Coast hinterland also promises some lovely aesthetics and a scattering of attractions, from the fast-growing Australia Zoo – home of the late 'Crocodile Hunter' Steve Irwin – and the waterfalls, coastal views and cosy

B&Bs of the Blackall Range, to the world-renowned art and craft markets at Eumundi.

North of the Noosa River, the coastal strip gives way to the vast expanses of the Great Sandy Region. Again, this region is aptly named. For thousands of years, ocean currents have steadily deposited the sediments washed out from the watersheds of the Great Dividing Range to form the largest coastal sand mass in the world. The Cooloola section of the Great Sandy National Park features vast swathes

Alexandria Bay, Noosa National Park

of ancient coloured sands, freshwater lakes and abundant wildlife. However, for all its assets it offers only a taste of something even bigger and better to come. Fraser Island – the largest coastal sand island in the world – is unquestionably the most popular tourist attraction in southern Queensland and certainly one of the most beautiful. With its unique and often unexpected range of habitats, natural features and rich biodiversity, all of which can only be explored by 4WD, Fraser Island presents a unique and remarkable eco-experience.

The main gateway and stepping stone to Fraser is the fast-growing coastal town of Hervey Bay. Though principally the domain of the retiree, between the months of July and October it can accurately declare itself the whale-watching capital of Australia.

Sunshine and Fraser coasts (see p80 for orange route excursion)

MOOLOOLABA, MAROOCHYDORE AND NOOSA

Mooloolaba and Maroochydore

100km (62 miles) north of Brisbane

As you might expect, the principal focus of activity in the two southern resort towns of the Sunshine Coast centres around the beach. However, in Mooloolaba, the harbour and wharf offer cruising, diving, fishing and kayaking. **Underwater World** also offers a fine introduction to Queensland's aquatic creatures, from delicate sea dragons to toothy crocodiles (*Parklyn Parade. Tel: (07) 5458 6222. www.underwaterworld.com.au. Open: 9am–5pm. Admission charge*). The highlight is an 80m (262ft) transparent tunnel that burrows through a huge oceanarium containing over 20,000 fish, including patrolling sharks.

In Maroochydore, the **Maroochy River** is the big attraction, offering a range of water activities, from waterskiing to kayaking. The river is also home to dozens of resident black swans and indeed the name 'Maroochydore' is thought to have derived from the Aboriginal words 'marutchi' and 'murukutchidha', which combined mean 'waters of the black swans'. The **Maroochy Waters Wetlands Sanctuary** features boardwalks through melaleuca swamps and mangroves that fringe the river. It can be reached from Sports Rd, Bli Bli.

Maroochy Visitor Information Centre. Corner of First Ave & Brisbane Rd. Tel: (07) 5459 9050. www.maroochytourism.com.au. Open: Mon–Sun 9am–5pm.

Private jetties and boats abound at Mooloolaba

The main beach at Noosa

Noosa

134km (83 miles) north of Brisbane
Noosa refers to a string of barely separated settlements that border the Noosa River and fringe the Noosa Heads National Park. From the east along the southern bank of the Noosa River, the mainly residential, low-key communities of Tewantin and Noosaville connect with each other and Noosa Heads, the focus for tourism, at the western fringe of Noosa Heads National Park. To the south of the park Sunshine Beach sits facing the ocean, east of Noosa Junction. With so many vague boundaries to these settlements, finding your way around the area is difficult and made worse by a seemingly endless string of roundabouts and inland waterways, so come armed with an area map. There is no denying the beauty or the class of Noosa, but one can't help thinking it yet another east-coast town that has become a victim of its own success and is now thoroughly lost to popularity and the dollar. One only needs to stroll along its main drag **Hastings St** in Noosa Heads to realise it is only a matter of time before Gucci or Lacoste opens a boutique store, and the old days of Betty's Hamburgers and 'G'day mate' from a happy-go-lucky local surfer are long gone.

That said, the simple aesthetics and the wealth of activities on offer will make sure you won't be disappointed here. You can be as relaxed or as pampered as you like, or take on anything from surfing lessons to camel treks. There are also plenty of attractions that will not require return trips to the cash machine. In addition to the sublime surf beach by Hastings St, the **Noosa National Park** beckons, with its coastal pathways, bays and resident koala.

Noosa Visitor Information Centre.
Hastings St, Noosa Heads.
Tel: 1300 066 672 & (07) 5430 5000.
www.tourismnoosa.com.au.
Open: 9am–5pm.

From big bananas to giant worms: Australia's 'Big Things' inventory

Where it all started remains something of an enigma, but there is no doubt that Australia's 'Big Things', as they are affectionately known, will add character and colour to your travels around Australia. There are currently around 160 of these weird and wonderful roadside edifices that adorn everything from town squares to restaurants nationwide in order to catch your attention. Of course the number varies, since big things come and big things go, but latest figures suggest that New South Wales has about 53 (the largest of any state), while Queensland has 44.

Some would have you believe it all started 40 years ago with an 11m (36ft) concrete banana in Coffs Harbour, but others would disagree.

Maybe it was the Big Mango in Bowen? Or the Big Mower in Beerwah? Or how about the Big Meat Pie in Yatala? Surely you'd be a Big Macadamia Nut (in Nambour) to think otherwise? You could always ask the Big Scotsman in Adelaide, or the Big Miner in Ballarat, after all he's a Big Galah (Kimba) with a mouth like a Big Pelican (Noosa). Mind you, Big Ned Kelly in Maryborough says it's a lot of Big Bull (Rockhampton).

So, just to make sure, my little (Big) Pumpkin (in Beaudesert), catch a Big Rig in Roma, or better still, jump on a Big Bike in Southport, head past the Big Mandarin in Munduberra and the Big Gumboot in Tully to get to the Big Gold Panner in Bathurst. He'll know, surely. Then, if he is off trying to catch a Big Murray Cod in Tocumwal, get on the Big Mobile

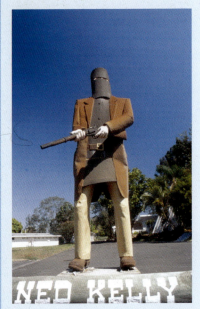

The notorious bushranger (highwayman) Ned Kelly at Maryborough, Queensland

The Big Banana at Coffs Harbour

Phone in Hurstville to ask Big Santa in Macksville.

Go on… you Big Chicken (Moonbi).

East Coast 'Big Things'
In your travels from Sydney to Cairns, keep a look out for the following well-known Big Things. They're pretty hard to miss.

In New South Wales Big Bottle (Pokolbin, Hunter Valley); Big Bowl and Big Eight Ball (Port Macquarie); Big Banana and Big Windmill (Coffs Harbour); Big Prawn (Ballina); Big Joint (Nimbin); Big Avocado (Tweed Heads).

In Queensland Big Frog (Brisbane Airport); Big Pelican (Noosa); Big Shell and Big Stubby (Tewantin); Big Boomerang and Big Sticks (Eumundi); Big Cow and Big Macadamia Nut (Nambour); Big Merino (Blackall); Big Mower (Beerwah); Big Rum Bottle and Big Turtle (Bundaberg); Big Bull, Big Crab and Big Dugong (Rockhampton); Big Cane Toad (Sarina); Big Mango (Bowen); Big Brolga (Townsville); Big Crab (Cardwell); Big Gumboot (Tully); Big Cassowary (Mission Beach); Big Marlin and Big Captain Cook (Cairns); Big Crocodile (Hartley's Creek); Big Barramundi (Daintree).

Drive: Noosa hinterland and the Blackall Range

This scenic drive explores the Noosa hinterland and in particular the Blackall Range, known for its pretty villages and spectacular views of the coast and the Glass House Mountains.

Allow a whole day for this 175km (109-mile) drive. Note the Eumundi markets and Australia Zoo each take up to a half-day to explore, so you may wish to choose one or the other, or allow two days for the trip.

From Noosa Heads take the SH12 southwest to Eumundi (17km/10½ miles).

1 Eumundi and the markets

For over 30 years now the pretty hinterland village of Eumundi has hosted what has become one of the premier arts and crafts markets in Australia. The markets offer a creative extravaganza of over 500 stalls selling everything from homemade soaps to bandanas. There are numerous food outlets as well.
Tel: (07) 5442 7106. Open: Wed 8am–1.30pm, Sat 6.30am–2pm
From Eumundi head south on the M1 (Bruce Highway) taking the Nambour exit to Mapleton (30km/19 miles).

2 Mapleton

The ascent into Mapleton opens up the first of many views back towards the coast. Nearby, the Mapleton Falls National Park is worth a quick look. The 120m (390ft) falls can be accessed 2½km (1½ miles) west on Obi Obi Rd. Nearby, the 1.3km (¾-mile) Wompoo Circuit walk winds through rainforest and eucalypts, providing excellent views of the Obi Obi Valley.
Return to Mapleton and head south to Montville (10km/6 miles).

3 Montville

With its European-style historic buildings, cosy cafés, art galleries and souvenir shops, the historic village provides the ideal stop for lunch or a stroll. Nearby, Lake Baroon is a pleasant picnic spot.
From Montville continue south and then west, taking in the coastal views to Maleny (15km/9½ miles).

4 Maleny

This small town has some interesting arts and crafts galleries and a winery.
At the far end of town turn left down the narrow Maleny-Stanley Rd to access Mountain View Rd (3km/2 miles).

5 Glass House Mountains

Heading back towards the coast, you are almost immediately offered the first stunning views of the 13 volcanic peaks from McCarthy's Lookout. A few kilometres further on is the Mary Cairncross Scenic Reserve, the legacy of the eponymous 19th-century environmentalist. The park has a small environmental centre and a short, pleasant rainforest walk.

From the Cairncross Reserve the road descends through the Blackall Range towards Landsborough. From Landsborough head south on SH60 towards Beerwah (6km/3¾ miles).

6 Australia Zoo

Once an innocuous wildlife sanctuary, the Australia Zoo now hosts over a million visitors a year, a result of the hype and exposure of the late 'Crocodile Hunter' (alias Steve Irwin), to whom the zoo was official home base. The top-class facility houses a wide array of well-maintained displays exhibiting over 550 native and non-native species, from insomniac wombats to huge pythons. But the main draw is the crocodile feeding that is enthusiastically demonstrated daily at 1pm.

Tel: (07) 5436 2000.
www.crocodilehunter.com.au.
Open: 9am–4.30pm. Admission charge.
From Beerwah head back north via SH60 to the M1 (Bruce Highway) and back to Noosa (72km/45 miles).

Drive: Noosa hinterland and the Blackall Range

NOOSA TO HERVEY BAY
Great Sandy National Park
(Cooloola)

144km (89 miles) north of Noosa
Given time constraints and the 70km (45-mile) diversion from SH1, the vast majority of tourists miss out the Cooloola Coast section of the Great Sandy National Park and instead press on to reach Fraser Island via Hervey Bay. However, a 4WD exploration of this unspoiled region can prove a rewarding experience. The most remarkable features of the 56,000ha (138,380-acre) park are its ancient coloured sands, huge sand blows and weathered wrecks, all of which can be explored by a network of 4WD tracks and walking trails. Other popular activities include wildlife-watching, horse-trekking and fishing. There are several designated campsites, and permits are required.

The park can be accessed from the south via Noosa (4WD only) and from the fast-developing seaside village of Rainbow Beach at the northern end of the park. Rainbow Beach is also used as a stepping stone to Fraser Island and, along with Tin Can Bay to the west, offers the rare opportunity to feed wild dolphins.

The **QPWS (Queensland Parks and Wildlife Service)** offices in Rainbow Beach (*Rainbow Beach Rd. Tel: (07) 5486 3160*) or Tewantin (*240 Moorindil St, Tewantin, Noosa. Tel: (07) 5449 7792*) have detailed information and issue camping permits (*both offices open: 7am–4pm*).

Hervey Bay

290km (180 miles) north of Brisbane
Considered the whale-watching capital of Australia, Hervey Bay tries hard to stand alone as an attractive coastal resort and congenial retirement destination. Yet outside the whale season (June–Oct), it struggles to keep people on the mainland for anything other than a day or night stocking up or sorting out the logistics of their great Fraser Island adventure. The city is essentially a beachfront conglomerate of north-facing suburbs. Almost all major amenities are to be found along the Esplanade from the junction with

A view along Noosa beach

A humpback whale puts on a display at Hervey Bay

Main St in Pialba to Elizabeth St in Urangan. The main Fraser Island ferry and whale-watching terminal is just south of Dayman Point in Urangan. There are numerous whale- and dolphin-watching cruise options available, from half-day catamaran to a full-day under sail.

The two **Visitor Information Centres** offer the best impartial advice:

Maryborough Fraser Island VIC. City Hall, Kent St, Maryborough. Tel: (07) 4190 5742. www.visitmaryborough.info. Open: 9am–5pm. Hervey Bay VIC. 1km (²/₃ mile) before Hervey Bay (signposted), Maryborough/Hervey Bay Rd. Tel: (07) 4125 9855. www.visitherveybay.info. Open: 9am–5pm.

STEVE IRWIN (CROCODILE HUNTER)

The concept of white male Australian meets native Australian wildlife has always provided the world's media with highly popular and sensational material, from Rolf Harris to the *Crocodile Dundee* blockbuster films starring Paul Hogan in the 1980s. But in recent years it was the exuberant and often controversial antics of TV celebrity and showman Steve Irwin – the 'Crocodile Hunter' – that proved iconic, particularly in the USA. Underpinning his worldwide TV appearances and ultimate success was the element of danger and his close encounters with dangerous wildlife. However, many saw his modus operandi as deeply disturbing and ultimately doing the public perception of wildlife more harm than good.

Based at his highly successful Australia Zoo, originally founded by his father near Brisbane, Steve and Terri Irwin created a commercial empire, complete with speaking dolls and clothing lines named after their first child, Bindi. Then, in late 2006, at the very peak of his celebrity career and while filming on the Great Barrier Reef, Steve was killed by a stingray. For many it was Australia's 'Diana moment'. For others, however, along with the sympathy there was also a quiet sigh of relief on behalf of the nation's wildlife. Although his true legacy remains to be seen, a big part of that will no doubt be Bindi, who now looks on course to inherit her father's celebrity status.

Excursion: Fraser Island

This flexible multi-day trip explores the stunning natural features of Fraser Island, which, at 162,600ha (401,790 acres), is the world's largest sand island. At 800,000 years old and home to a rich and unique biodiversity, Fraser Island is part of the World Heritage-listed Great Sandy National Park. The only way to explore its extensive beaches, hidden lakes and remarkably lofty forests is by 4WD vehicle.

Allow two or three days (around 400km/248 miles).

Wanggoolba Creek to East Beach is about 20km (12½ miles).

1 East Beach

Driving along the entire 121km (75-mile) natural highway of East Beach is an exhilarating experience in itself. The main access point for those arriving from the west coast is Eurong. There are a number of sights as you head north from there, the first of which is Lake Wabby, 4km (2½ miles) north of Eurong. Reached by foot, Lake Wabby is partly inundated by a natural sand blow, creating bizarre aesthetics and lots of sand-surfing and swimming fun. Next stop is Eli Creek, one of the island's few natural streams, offering a cool dip. Some 3km (2 miles) beyond Eli Creek is the iconic rusting hulk of the *Maheno*, a small passenger liner that came to grief in 1935.

Beyond some colourful sand banks, continue to Indian Head. One of the very few genuine rocks on the island, it offers a fine vantage point. Just beyond, at the start of Middle Head, the track turns inland before delivering you to Orchid Beach and the perfect saltwater swimming venue, the Champagne Pools.

2 The lakes

There are over 40 freshwater lakes on Fraser, with the most popular and stunning scattered around the island's southern interior. By far the most beautiful (and visited) is Lake McKenzie, 9km (5½ miles) north of Central Station. With its white silica sands and crystal-clear waters, it is the highlight for many visitors and the perfect place to cool off.

3 Central Station

As the name suggests, Central Station is in the heart of the island (21km/ 13 miles from Eurong). Here, the 50m (164ft) canopies of towering bunya pine are complemented by thick umbrella-like palms and the white sandy bed of the Wanggoolba Creek. Central Station also serves as the

departure point for some excellent
walking tracks to Lake McKenzie.

GETTING THERE
AND AROUND

By far the best way to experience Fraser
Island is to hire your own 4WD. There are
numerous hire outlets in Hervey Bay.
Vehicular access is from Hervey Bay
(Urangan) to Moon Point and Kingfisher
Bay; River Head (20 minutes south of Hervey
Bay) to Kingfisher Bay and Wanggoolba
Creek; and from Rainbow Beach (Inskip
Point) to Hook Point, the southernmost tip
of the Island. Another alternative is to fly to
the island, hire a 4WD on arrival and then
take the ferry back to the mainland. Many
alternatives and packages are available (see
below). All vehicles require a Vehicle Service
Permit before arrival.

Accommodation

There is limited accommodation on the
island to suit all budgets, including the multi-
award-winning **Kingfisher Bay Resort**
(*Tel: (07) 4125 5511. www.kingfisherbay.com*).
The QPWS has designated campsites
throughout the island, some with coin-
operated hot showers.

Information

For all details, contact **Hervey Bay Visitor
Information Centre** (*1km/²⁄₃ mile before
Hervey Bay (signposted), off Maryborough/
Hervey Bay Rd. Tel: (07) 4125 9855.
www.visitherveybay.info. Open: 9am–5pm*).
QPWS offices on the mainland and island
can also assist. *Tel: (07) 4127 9128.
www.epa.qld.gov.au*

   The island has a complex network of sand
tracks and, although most routes are clearly
signposted, it is essential to carry a detailed
map. The 1:130,000 Fraser Island Tourist
Map is very detailed (available from the
Visitor Information Centre, QPWS offices
and local newsagents).

Capricorn and central Queensland coasts

After the great sand masses of the Fraser Coast, tourist attentions turn offshore to the southernmost islands of the Great Barrier Reef. From the Capricornia Cays, the world's largest single living entity begins to state its fragmented and colourful presence for the next 2,600km (1,600 miles) north all the way to Cape York.

Back on dry land is the first of many Queensland towns borne of the sugar cane industry: Bundaberg. Although aesthetically unremarkable, it is famous for its fascinating rum distillery.

On the coast near Bundaberg, the beach at Mon Repos (French for 'my place of rest') has served for centuries as one of the world's most important and accessible mainland turtle rookeries. Under the careful watch of wardens and the visiting public these ancient, determined creatures return annually to lay dozens of eggs deep in the sand. Weeks later small battalions of babies emerge and charge like crazed clockwork miniatures to the safety of the surf.

Further north is the historic coastal 'Town of 1770', the first place Captain Cook (and effectively Europeans) first set foot in Queensland. Along with its small and equally fast-developing neighbour Agnes Waters, it serves as the gateway to the stunning southern reef island Lady Musgrave.

Next up is the coastal port of Gladstone. Due to its stark industrial aesthetics, it is usually missed by tourists, bar those lucky individuals en route to the popular and luxury Barrier Reef resort of Heron Island. Just to the north of Gladstone you cross the Tropic of Capricorn to Queensland's 'beef capital', Rockhampton. Many visitors make their stay in Rockhampton a brief one in favour of the coastal resort of Yeppoon or Great Keppel Island.

Mackay is roughly halfway between Brisbane and Cairns and presents its own quality regional and natural attractions in the form of the Eungella and Cape Hillsborough national parks.

Again offshore, never far from the horizon, is the Barrier Reef and its myriad islands, a paradise for sailing and diving. Off Airlie Beach the Whitsunday Islands are arguably the country's most popular conglomerate, replete with wilderness and a scattering of resorts, some of which seem straight from the set of a James Bond film.

Capricorn and central Queensland coasts
(see p104 for orange route drive)

Lizard Island

Cooktown

Cape Tribulation
Daintree
Mossman

CAIRNS
Cairns

Fitzroy Island

Tully
Mission Beach
Dunk Island

Cardwell
Hinchinbrook Island NP
Hinchinbrook Island

Orpheus Island

Greenvale

Coral Sea

GREAT BARRIER REEF

Magnetic Island

Townsville International
TOWNSVILLE

Mingela

Charters Towers

Ravenswood

Collinsville

Bowen
Whitsunday Islands
Airlie Beach
Proserpine

Cape Hillsborough NP

Eungella NP
Eungella
Eimeo
Mackay

Mount Coolon

Yarrowmere

Sarina
Oxford Downs

Moranbah

Northumberland Isles

QUEENSLAND

Aramac

Tropic of Capricorn

Barcaldine

Emerald

Marlborough
Rydges Capricorn Resort
Rockhampton

Byfield NP

Great Keppel Island
Yeppoon
Heron Island

Lady Musgrave Island

Springsure

Gladstone
Eurimbula NP
Miriam Vale
Town of 1770
Agnes Waters
Deepwater NP

Blackall

Caldervale

Bundaberg
Mon Repos
Turtle Rookery

Maryborough
Fraser Island

Taroom

Injune

Gympie
Tin Can Bay

Charleville
Muckadilla
Roma

Landsborough
Tewantin
Moreton Island

Surat

Dalby

Boatman

Toowoomba
Brisbane International
BRISBANE

St George

Gold Coast

Cunnamulla

Goondiwindi

City
Large Town
Small Town
Start of Drive
POI
Main Road
Minor Road
Airport
Railway

0   200km
0   100 miles

From Airlie, the seemingly never-ending Bruce Highway delivers you in Townsville, Queensland's second-largest city. As well as having its own quality attractions, it serves as a base from which to venture 'outback' to the former gold-mining boom town of Charters Towers, while just offshore Magnetic Island is yet another fine venue for all things sun and surf.

Finally, with Cairns reachable in one day, it would be rude not to first experience the tropical delights of Mission Beach or Dunk Island, where with a little luck you may encounter that huge avian 'black wig on legs', the cassowary.

Bundaberg

385km (240 miles) north of Brisbane, 326km (202 miles) south of Rockhampton 40km (25 miles) towards the coast from the Bruce Highway the agricultural service town of Bundaberg sits amid a sea of sugar cane and is world famous for one thing: rum. Not surprisingly, the 1883 **Bundaberg Distillery** is the biggest tourist attraction and tours provide a fascinating insight into the distilling process (*Avenue St, 4km/2¹/2 miles east of the city centre, head for the chimney stack. Tel: (07) 4131 2990. www.bundabergrum.com.au. Tours: on the hour Mon–Fri 10am–3pm, Sat & Sun 10am–2pm. Admission charge).* Though a little heavy with its promotion of the brand itself, it provides a delightful bombardment of the senses from the sweet smell of

Dark and Stormy, one of the Bundaberg Distillery's many fine brews

molasses to the inevitable titillation of the taste buds sampling the end product.

From tipple to turtle... It's a strange combination, but the other main attraction in these parts is the **Mon Repos Turtle Rookery** 12km (7¹/2 miles) east of the city (*Grange Rd, off Bundaberg Port Rd. Tel: (07) 4159 1652. www.epa.qld.gov.au. Information centre open: 24 hrs (Oct–May); 6am–6pm (June–Sept). Turtle viewing: 7pm–6am (Oct–May, subject to activity). Admission charge).* Supporting one of the largest loggerhead turtle rookeries in the world, this is one of the few places you can see the adults lay the eggs and the manic little hatchlings emerge from beneath the sand. All the remarkable action takes place after dark, with females laying between mid-October and May and the hatchlings emerging from January to March.

Bundaberg Visitor Information Centre. *271 Bourbong St. Tel: (07) 4153 8888. www.bundabergregion.org. Open: 9am–5pm.*

Agnes Water and The Town of 1770

140km (87 miles) north of Bundaberg
Agnes Water and The Town of 1770 are both undeniably beautiful, but they do possess very odd names. It was none other than Captain Cook who christened the latter on a visit in, well, guess when! These once sleepy, unspoiled coastal settlements have merged in recent years into a significant tourism destination in their own right, with beautiful local beaches, the Deepwater and Eurimbula national parks and access to **Lady Musgrave Island** 50km (31 miles) offshore being the great attractions. For many, a trip to Musgrave is their first real experience of the Barrier Reef.

1770 Environmental Tours offers some excellent trips aboard an

A hatchling loggerhead turtle at Mon Repos Turtle Rookery

amphibious vehicle to explore the diverse wildlife and habitats of the two national parks (*Tel: (07) 4974 9422. www.1770larctours.com.au*). **Lady Musgrave Barrier Reef Cruises** depart daily from The Town of 1770 (*Tel: 1800 072 110. www.lmcruises.com.au*).

For more information contact the **Discovery Centre** (*Captain Cook Dr, Agnes Water. Tel: (07) 4902 1533. Open: Mon–Sat 8.30am–5pm*).

Rockhampton

634km (394 miles) north of Brisbane
First settled in 1855 and boosted by a brief gold rush later that same decade, Rockhampton has steadily developed into a major agricultural service town and is labelled the 'beef capital' of Australia. Although most visitors stay only briefly on their way to the coastal resorts of Yeppoon and Great Keppel Island, 'Rocky' (as it is known) offers a diverse range of tourist attractions from the historical and cultural to the ecological and even subterranean in the form of the **Capricorn Caves**, some of the most accessible anywhere in Australia (*Olsen's Caves Rd. Tel: (07) 4934 2883. www.capricorncaves.com.au. Open: 9am–4pm. Admission charge*).

The **Rockhampton Visitor Information Centre** is housed in the grandiose 1902 Customs House (*208 Quay St. Tel (07) 4922 5339. www.rockhamptoninfo.com. Open: Mon–Fri 8.30am–4.30pm, Sat & Sun 9am–4pm*).

Yeppoon and Great Keppel Island

40km (25 miles) east of Rockhampton

The laid-back seaside town of Yeppoon and the string of pretty beaches to its south – Cooee and Rosslyn Bays, Kinka Beach and Emu Park – form the main focus of the Capricorn Coast and serve as the region's principal coastal holiday resorts.

Great Keppel Island, 15km (9 miles) offshore from Rosslyn Bay, is also a popular resort and the largest of a relatively undeveloped cluster of 18 islands making up the **Great Keppel Island National Park**.

There is plenty of accommodation all along the coast and on Great Keppel to suit all budgets and, other than all the usual water and beach-based activities, attractions include the vast coastal wilderness of the **Byfield National Park**, home to a rich variety of waterbirds and a popular venue for 4WD and horse-trekking.

The **Rydges Capricorn Resort** (9km/5½ miles north of Yeppoon) serves as a fine base from which to explore the national park and offers a wide range of organised activities (*Tel: 1300 857 922. www.rydges.com*).

There are regular ferries to Great Keppel from the Keppel Bay Marina at Rosslyn Bay Harbour, 7km (4⅓ miles) south of Yeppoon. **Freedom Fast Cats** offer transport only, or half- and full-day cruise/activity options (*Tel: (07) 4933 6244. www.keppelbaymarina.com.au. Ferries depart 9am, 11.30am & 3.30pm*).

For more details, contact the **Capricorn Region Visitor Information Centre** (*Gladstone Rd, Rockhampton. Tel: (07) 4927 2055. www.capricorntourism.com.au*).

One of Great Keppel Island's tranquil beaches

Mackay and Eungella National Park

334km (207 miles) north of Rockhampton
What Newcastle is to coal and the Hunter to wine, Mackay is to sugar, with the sea of cane fields that surround it now producing over a third of the nation's sweet stuff. First settled in 1860, it offers an intriguing mix of old and new, with 'the new' now transforming the place with ever-increasing vigour. Although the city is predominantly a service town, it does offer a few attractions within city limits, and within range are the Eungella and Cape Hillsborough national parks, arguably two of the state's best.

Artspace Mackay is a relatively recent addition to the city's 'new' portfolio and houses both an art gallery and museum (*Gordon St, Civic Centre Precinct. Tel: (07) 4957 1775. www.artspacemackay.com.au. Open: Tue–Sun 10am–5pm. Free admission*). The sugar industry features heavily but this is interspersed neatly with other more contemporary displays, including a pseudo shrine to the city's most famous daughter, Olympic gold-medal runner Cathy Freeman.

The 80km (50-mile) scenic drive from Mackay to the **Eungella National Park** (pronounced 'young-galah') offers a welcome break from the coast, with spectacular views and bush walks. Not to be missed are the walks and waterfalls in the Finch Hatton Gorge section of the park, the valley views

from the Eungella Chalet, and Broken River, where platypus can often be seen at dawn or dusk.

Just north of Mackay and in stark contrast, the small and coastal **Cape Hillsborough National Park** offers a fine break from the road. Apart from its beautiful rugged coastal scenery, it is also known for its resident population of roos, who are not averse to enjoying their own little paddle in the surf.

The **Mackay Visitor Information Centre** is located in a former sugar mill on the Bruce Highway (*320 Nebo Rd. Tel: 1300 130 001. www.mackayregion.com. Open: Mon–Fri 8.30am–5pm, Sat & Sun 9am–4pm.*)

Whitsunday Islands and Airlie Beach

153km (95 miles) north of Mackay
With over 74 sun-drenched tropical islands, the Whitsundays are not only the largest offshore island chain on the East Coast but the biggest tourist draw between Brisbane and Cairns. Like much of Queensland's idyllic coastline, this is a region where reality can meet expectation, where the very concept of tropical paradise so keenly hyped and promised by the glossy brochures actually comes true. The majority of the islands in the group are, thankfully, fully protected under the auspices of the Whitsunday Islands National Park, but since the 1930s some began to host holiday resorts. These resorts vary from the commercial apartment jungle on Hamilton Island to the

almost unimaginable luxuries of Hayman. Elsewhere, basic and sometimes remote island campsites offer a great opportunity to escape the crowds. But regardless of the budget, combined they offer a veritable paradise for sailing, diving or just lying on a beach with a good book.

The portal to the Whitsunday Islands is the highly commercial tourist town of Airlie Beach, with its myriad backpackers and man-made lagoon proving a buzzing social magnet. Many end up staying in Airlie Beach itself, lying by the lagoon, nursing hangovers, but given the accessibility of the island resorts, it is wise to do your homework before arrival and quickly get out among them. One of the best ways to do that is under sail on a multi-day live-aboard yacht. Prices vary according to vessel and activities but there is no end of choice.

Principal islands and resorts

Hamilton Island The most developed island and resort. Full range of accommodation, amenities and activities.

Hayman Island Quite simply superb. Home to an exclusive resort that looks straight out of the set of a Bond film. Take out a second mortgage though.

Hook Island Second-largest island, renowned for excellent snorkelling and

Looking out towards the Whitsunday Islands

Deserted bays and beaches are not hard to find around the Whitsunday Islands

diving on fringing coral reefs. Hosts a low-key resort and several campsites.
Long Island Long, narrow, forested island with mid- to top-range resorts including the remote South Long Island Wilderness Resort accessed only by helicopter.

The Molles and Daydream Island
Closet and most accessible to the mainland. Home to good mid-range resorts. South Molle also has some good walking tracks and is a worthwhile day visit option.

Whitsunday Island The largest of the group and home to **Whitehaven Beach**, one of the most beautiful and iconic in Australia. A visit to its almost surreal swathe of white sand is the main feature of most organised cruise trips.

Basic bush-camping is available. There is no resort. Gets very busy.

PRACTICALITIES

The islands are accessed by helicopter, fixed-wing aircraft or, most often, by ferries based at Shute Harbour 4km (2½ miles) south of Airlie Beach. Most resorts welcome day visitors and include transfers in their tariff. Numerous day-cruise packages and activity options are available. **Fantasea Cruises** are the main players (*Tel: (07) 4946 5111. www.fantasea.com.au*).

The main **Visitor Information Centre** is in Proserpine (*Bruce Highway. Tel: 1800 801 252. www.whitsundaytourism.com*).

The **QPWS office** can supply the latest island camping information and issue the necessary permits (*Shute Harbour Rd, Airlie Beach. Tel: (07) 4946 7022. Open: Mon–Fri 9am–5pm, Sat 9am–1pm*).

A farm surrounded by sugar cane near Townsville

Townsville

390km (242 miles) northwest of Mackay,
345km (214 miles) south of Cairns

First settled in 1864 to service the
regional cattle industry, it was the
discovery of gold inland at Ravenswood
and Charters Towers four years later that
accelerated Townsville's development
and put it firmly on the map. Like
Brisbane, it is often labelled the 'tropical
city' and is the second-largest in the state.

Although agriculture still plays the
predominant role in the local economy,
tourism is important, with several
high-profile city attractions and the
proximity of Magnetic Island – one of
the most accessible and popular of the
state's tropical islands – securing a
steady stream of domestic and
international visitors. Many diving
enthusiasts also come here to
experience what is often touted as
the best wreck dive in Australia in the
diminished form of the SS *Yongala*,
a passenger ship that sank off Cape
Bowling Green with the loss of all 121
crew – and a racehorse called
Moonshine – during a cyclone in 1911.

Billabong Wildlife Sanctuary

Just 17km (10½ miles) south of the
city, this is one of the best wildlife
exhibits on the East Coast. It offers a far
less manic atmosphere than most parks
of its ilk and has all the usual suspects,
including the extraordinary and leggy
cassowary. There are various shows and
talks throughout the day, some of
which give you the opportunity to
handle the more docile snakes and
baby crocs.

Bruce Highway. Tel: (07) 4778 8344.
www.billabongsanctuary.com.au.
Open: 8am–5pm. Admission charge.

Museum of Queensland

Located next door to Reef HQ, this modern museum provides an impressive insight into the region's social and maritime history, with the story of HMS *Pandora*, the British 17th-century tall ship associated with the more infamous HMS *Bounty*, predominating. There is also an interactive science centre to keep the kids and the less nautically inclined suitably engaged.

Flinders St East. Tel: (07) 4726 0606. www.mtq.qld.gov.au. Open: 9.30am–5pm. Admission charge.

Reef HQ

Offers an excellent land-based introduction to the reef's multifarious 'who's who' from the big, the small, the poisonous and the beautiful to the downright ugly. Centrepiece within the facility is a huge 750,000-litre 'Predator Exhibit' that comes with genuine wave action. As you would expect, sharks feature heavily, with feeding taking place on most days at 3pm.

2–68 Flinders St East. Tel: (07) 4750 0800. www.reefHQ.org.au.
Open: 9.30am–5pm. Admission charge.

Magnetic Island

Only 12km (7½ miles) off Townsville and blessed with an extensive national park, numerous secluded bays and beautiful beaches, it is little wonder Magnetic Island – named by Captain Cook in 1770 – is one of the most popular island resorts on the Queensland coast. Several small and pleasant tourist-based communities admirably service visitors with a wide range of accommodation and activities from diving to bush-walking. The island is noted for its resident koala population. There are regular ferry services from Townsville to Nelly Bay.

Visit the main **Visitor Information Centre** for details (*Bruce Highway, 7km (4¼ miles) south of the town. Tel: (07) 4778 3555. www.townsvilleonline.com.au. Open: 9am–5pm*).

Information booths are also to be found in **Flinders Mall** (*Tel: (07) 4721 3660. Open: Mon–Fri 9am–5pm, Sat & Sun 9am–1pm*) and next to the **Museum of Queensland** (*70–102 Flinders St East. Tel: (07) 4721 1116. Open: 9am–5pm*).

The snake show at Billabong Wildlife Sanctuary

Drive: Outback to Ravenswood and Charters Towers

This drive offers the coast-weary traveller a welcome change in the 'outback', where in the 1860s the discovery of gold turned a nondescript rocky outcrop into the second-largest city in Queensland. See page 95 for map.

Allow a whole day for this 346km (215-mile) drive.

From Townsville take the A6 southwest of the city. At Mingela (88km/55 miles along the A6) follow signs south (left) to Ravenswood.

1 Ravenswood

Amid the shimmering heat, the lonely buildings and silence, it is hard to

Relics litter old properties in the former gold-mining town of Ravenswood

believe that the now sleepy village of Ravenswood was once the chaotic home of over 700 manic, hopeful souls who, with the discovery of gold at the nearby Elphinstone Creek, came here to seek their fortune. Of course, for the vast majority it never happened and within a few decades they were gone.

Today a few old buildings remain, including two of what used to be over fifty hotel taverns. There is also a small museum in the former **Court House** (*Tel: (07) 4770 2047. Open: 10am–3pm. Closed: Tue. Admission charge*).
Return to the A6 and continue southwest to Charters Towers (47km/29 miles).

2 Charters Towers

The rather grand town of Charters Towers has a fascinating history. Once the second-largest city in the state and nicknamed 'The World' thanks to its cosmopolitan population, it effectively owes its existence to an Aboriginal boy named Jupiter. It was young Jupiter who in 1871 stumbled across the first gold-encrusted quartz while looking for lost horses. After presenting it to his boss, the rest is history. Within a year the area was home to over 3,000. The boom lasted until around 1917, by which time over $25 million worth of the precious metal had been extracted. The town derives its name from Mr Charters, the mining warden who registered the Mosman (Jupiter's boss) claim located near Towers Hill.

The town has some fine old buildings, including the 1888 former **Stock Exchange Building** and, next door, the aesthetically magnificent, former **Australian Bank of Commerce** of 1892. Combined, they now host the **World Theatre Complex**, a gallery, café and an assay room filled with mining artefacts, including a working model of a stamping battery (*Tel: (07) 4787 4337. Open: Mon–Fri 8.30am–4.30pm, Sat & Sun 9am–3pm. Admission charge*).

Other heritage buildings and points of interest in the city include the **Miner's Cottage** on Deane St; the 1892 **Post Office** and 1910 **Police Station** on Gill St; the 1882 **Pfeiffer House** on Paul St; and the interior of the 1886 **Civic Club** on Ryan St.

On the outskirts of the city (east via Gill St and Millchester Rd), the **Venus Gold Battery** is worth a visit. The battery, built in 1872, remains in very good condition and is the largest surviving battery relic in Australia. Interpretive displays present the process of extracting the gold from quartz.

The 1888 World Theatre, Charters Towers

Guided tours can be booked through the Visitor Information Centre (*see below*).

If you have time, it is worth calling in to see if there is any action at the **Dalrymple Sale Yards** just south of the city on Flinders Highway. They are one of the largest stock sale yards in the region.

Towers Hill (420m/1,380ft) provides excellent views across the city and beyond (*Access via south end of Mosman St, off Black Jack Rd*).

And what happened to Jupiter? History suggests that the reward for his find was adoption by Mosman and an 'education in the European manner'.

The **Visitor Information Centre** is housed in the former band hall building between the former Stock Exchange and City Hall (*74 Mosman St. Tel: (07) 4752 0314. www.charterstowers.qld.gov.au. Open: 9am–5pm*).

Hinchinbrook Island National Park

At 40,000ha (98,840 acres), lying 4km (2½ miles) offshore from Cardwell, this is Australia's largest island national park and one of the largest in the world. Crowned by the 1,142m (3,746ft) Mount Bowen and replete with untainted native bush, pristine beaches and fascinating flora and fauna, it is also one of the most beautiful. The island is uninhabited except for one small, low-key eco-resort which, along with the famed and popular 32km (20-mile) five-day Thorsborne Trail, forms the main focus of tourism activity. With the island's harsh topography, the trail is considered 'challenging'. Book the trail well in advance, as limited numbers are allowed at any one time.

The **QPWS Rainforest and Reef Centre** beside the jetty in Cardwell makes bookings, issues permits,

Vehicles have taken a heavy toll on the endangered cassowary

SLOW DOWN – BIG BIRD ON THE ROAD

Many are familiar with the Australian emu, or the African ostrich, but few are aware of that other great avian 'wig on legs', the cassowary. Like its lofty and leggy cousins, the cassowary is flightless and could certainly put in an eyebrow-raising spectacle at the finals of the Olympic 100m. Native to northern Australia and sadly now endangered, one of the few population hot spots is in the protected forest plantations surrounding Mission Beach. Despite their size, they are no match for vehicles and many are killed or injured on the region's roads annually. So, heed the road signs, slow down, and you might be rewarded with the sight of a vigilant mother herding her 'mini wigs' across the road.

trailhead and resort transfers, and can provide details of day cruises (*Bruce Highway. Tel: (07) 4066 8601. www.epa.qld.gov.au. Open: 8.30am–4.30pm*).

Mission Beach

In their eagerness to reach Cairns (120km/75 miles away), many people miss the small settlement of Mission Beach, which is a mistake. Located 74km (46 miles) north of Cardwell, with 14km (nearly 9 miles) of archetypal tropical coastline complete with coconut palms and offshore islands, it has plenty to offer. As yet, it lacks the crass commercialism of the Cairns region. Surrounded by national park, Mission Beach is noted for its flora and fauna. The intriguing stands of umbrella-like Licuala Palms and the bizarre and endangered avian resident, the cassowary, are the undisputed

Dunk Island's idyllic tropical beach

highlights. This is also a great spot to see the surreally beautiful, iridescent Ulysses Blue butterfly.

There's plenty of accommodation to suit all budgets, good facilities and a wealth of activities, including beach skydiving and day cruises. Ferry services leave regularly to the equally stunning Dunk Island (*see below*).

Ferry bookings and further information are available at the **Tourist Information Centre and Wet Tropics Environmental Centre** (*El-Arish-Mission Beach Rd, Porter Promenade. Tel: (07) 4068 7099. www.missionbeachtourism.com. Open: 9am–5pm*).

Dunk Island

5km (3 miles) offshore from Mission Beach
Beauty aside, sheer ease of access makes a visit to 'Dunk' a very attractive proposition. The sublime 730ha (1,800-acre) national and marine park has a high-profile, mid-range resort that welcomes day visitors, and there are over 14km (nearly 9 miles) of walking tracks. One of the most popular and challenging of these climbs through lush native bush to the island's highest point, Mount Kootaloo (271m/889ft).

AN ISLAND TO DIE FOR

In 1897 at the age of 46, one Edmund Banfield was diagnosed with a terminal illness and decided to live out his final days on Dunk Island. He died 26 years later, after writing *Confessions of a Beachcomber*, a national bestseller and a celebrated text for escapists, hopeless romantics and, no doubt, medical students.

Cairns and the far north

Far north Queensland has one of the richest biodiversities on earth and it is these extraordinary natural assets that form the foundation of its booming tourism industry. Unlike the rest of the parched continent, rain is no stranger here, with rainfall on Mount Bartle Frere (at 1,622m/ 5,320ft, the state's highest mountain) measured in metres. This liberal seasonal watering sustains vast tracks of lush World Heritage-listed rainforest covering almost 1 million ha (2,471,000 acres) from Cooktown to Townsville.

Believed to be over 100 million years in the making, the forest is also one of the oldest in the world, possessing the greatest single concentration of primitive flowering plants.

If all that were not enough, lying just offshore is the Great Barrier Reef. Stretching almost 2,600km (1,615 miles)

Cairns Lagoon Complex, now the city's favourite fair-weather venue

from Cape York to Bundaberg, it is the planet's largest single structure made by living organisms and, like the rainforest, sustains an almost unimaginable number and variety of species.

Not surprising, then, that the 'Wet Tropics Region' offers more to see and do than any other in Australia, and that Cairns is second only to Sydney for international visitor arrivals.

Having already been put firmly on the map by the discovery of gold in the region in the 1870s, it was the advent of the aqualung in the 1940s that proved to be Cairns' true 'Eureka'. Strategically positioned and already supporting a suitable deepwater harbour, its destiny as the gateway to the reef was sealed seemingly overnight. Now a thriving, if seasonal, tourist town, there is no end of fine accommodation, eateries, shops and activities, with the reef taking top billing. But amid all the hype and mania, it is perhaps too easy to lose sight of what it is that really sustains it all: unspoiled nature! To that end, many seek solace further north in the smaller and prettier coastal town of Port Stephens, or try to lose the crowds altogether in Daintree and Cape Tribulation, where the reef and rainforest are separated only by the tide.

West of Cairns, the lush, green plateau of the Atherton Tablelands also offers a cool retreat from the coast, with the arts-oriented rainforest village of Kuranda being its main attraction.

But whatever your intention, thankfully it is still nature that rules around here and she will hopefully always call the shots. When the mercury rises, the humidity becomes almost unbearable and the clouds gather during 'the wet' (Nov–Mar), it doesn't matter how many hotels you build and how plush the ensuite – the place will, once again and for a few months, become a ghost town.

Cairns and the far north

Cairns

1,703km (1,058 miles) north of Brisbane

A word of warning: you will have heard a lot about Cairns and will no doubt expect even more! Those expectations will include a great choice of accommodation, classy restaurants, good shopping and an atmosphere that only fuels a burning desire to experience the reef. Well, no problems there. The problem is that by now you have probably grown so accustomed to world-class beaches that you feel every east-coast Australian town should have one. Alas, to its eternal detriment, Cairns does not. Built on an estuary, here mud rules the shore. But they did try. In the late 1990s some bright spark suggested importing vast amounts of sand and, remarkably, the city fathers went with the idea. It looked marvellous for a few months, until the first cyclone dutifully took it back to whence it came.

Undaunted, bright sparks were revitalised (and re-employed) and in mortal hindsight came up with what has become Cairns' top land-based attraction: its very own manmade waterfront **Lagoon Complex**. Costing nothing (to visit that is) and strategically placed near the town centre, it has become the social hub of the town. It is the perfect spot to cool off, sunbathe and bury yourself in a mound of activity and reef cruises leaflets.

For all the logistical details, head for the accredited **Tourism Tropical**

The Esplanade in Cairns city centre

North Queensland Gateway
Discovery Centre (*51 The Esplanade.*
Tel: (07) 4051 3588.
www.tropicalaustralia.com.au.
Open: 8.30am–5.30pm).

Cairns Regional Art Gallery
Housed in the former 1936 Public
Curator's Offices, this worthwhile gallery
showcases mainly local and regional art
as well as national visiting exhibitions.
Corner of Abbott St & Shields St.
Tel: (07) 4046 4800.
www.cairnsregionalgallery.com.au.
Open: Mon–Sat 10am–5pm, Sun 1–5pm.
Admission charge for adults.

Cairns Wildlife Dome
A short stroll from the Esplanade and
housed in the glass rooftop dome of the
Reef Hotel Casino is the Cairns Wildlife
Dome, a small native menagerie with
over 100 inmates from the ubiquitous
koala to blue-tongued lizard. Although
commercial, it remains a good
introduction to the region's rich and
varied wildlife.
Tel: (07) 4031 7250.
www.cairnsrainforestdome.com.au.
Open: 8am–6pm. Admission charge.

Centre of Contemporary Arts (CoCA)
The CoCA, guarded on the outside by
five man-sized jelly babies, is home to
three resident arts companies and also
hosts international exhibitions.
96 Abbot St. Tel: (07) 4050 9401.
www.coca.org.au. Open: Tue–Sat
10am–5pm. Free admission.

Reef Teach
In Cairns it seems as though every
attraction is merely a precursor to
that quintessential reef experience,
and if you know very little about the
reef you should certainly attend Reef
Teach. In essence it is an entertaining
two-hour lecture on the basics of the
reef's remarkable natural history,
conservation and fish and coral
identification. The exuberant staff
can also give some solid
recommendations on which reef
activities to choose.
14 Spence St. Tel: (07) 4031 7794.
www.reefteach.com.au. Show time:
Mon–Sat 6.30pm. Admission charge.

St Monica's Cathedral
If you have time, take a wander up to
183 Abbott St and St Monica's
Cathedral to see the unique stained-
glass windows known as the 'Creation
Design'. The huge and spectacularly
colourful display even includes the
Great Barrier Reef, complete with
tropical fish.
Admission by donation.

Tanks Art Centre
Certainly worth a muse is the Tanks
Art Centre on the northern outskirts
of the city. These former diesel storage
tanks are now used as exhibition and
performance space for the local arts
community.
46 Collins St. Tel: (07) 4032 6600.
Open: Mon–Fri 11am–4pm.
Free admission.

The Great Barrier Reef

Like most things Australian, the Great Barrier Reef is big – very big. Stretching 2,600km (1,615 miles) from Cape York to Fraser Island, it can be seen from space and comprises over 3,000 individual reefs and around 900 islands. It is also the planet's biggest single structure made by living organisms, and its largest reef system. In essence, the reef is made up of and built by billions of minute coral polyps – about 400 species – over millions of years. The reef is also capable of the single biggest orgasm in the natural world – but more about that later!

So that's the structure. Now for the inhabitants. If you were to form a comprehensive list, it would read like a veritable A-list of the beautiful, the

A scorpion fish, one of many colourful and highly decorated species found on the reef

bizarre and the 'Good Lord, you've got to be joking'. There are, for example, over 5,000 species of mollusc, 125 species of shark, 17 species of sea snake, 30 species of whale and dolphin, 9 seahorse species, 500 seaweeds, 215 birds, 2,200 known terrestrial plant species, 7 frogs... and the list goes on.

Then there are the fish, with over 1,600 makes and models. With names as evocative as Old Wife, Bucket Mouth, clown and fusilier, many are stunningly beautiful. Everyone knows the pretty orange-and-black striped clown fish immortalised by the film *Finding Nemo*. Then there is the huge potato cod that has a set of lips that would have a Miami plastic surgeon raise an eyebrow. And for just plain remarkably ugly, the stonefish is hard to beat.

The reef is also home to some very venomous species. The stonefish is one of the most poisonous fish species on earth, while the innocuous-looking cone shell could bring down a small elephant. Then there are the marine stingers, of which the box jellyfish is the most notorious. But generally speaking, like any human neighbourhood, the bad

Face to face with a painted crayfish

can be avoided with a little common sense and the reef's impressive poisonous inventory should in no way prevent you donning a set of flippers and a mask.

It all adds up to a burning desire to visit the miraculous world beneath the waves. And visit we do, with over 2 million estimated visitors a year worth an estimated 5 billion dollars to the Australian economy. In order to lay the foundations for the long-term protection of the reef, the government created the Great Barrier Reef Marine Park in 1975, and in 1981 it was afforded World Heritage status.

But there is a dark side. The reef remains under threat not only from the conventional issues of mass tourism, pollution and over-fishing. Mass coral bleaching due to rising ocean temperatures occurred in the summers of 1998, 2002 and 2006, and if global warming is not managed, coral bleaching is likely to become an annual occurrence. A draft report by the UN Intergovernmental Panel on Climate Change states that the Great Barrier Reef is at grave risk and will be 'functionally extinct' by 2030.

Now, back to that orgasm. Every year over a third of the reef's coral species reproduce sexually, and they do this during a mass spawning event, always at night, in November or December, up to six days after a full moon. Eggs and sperm are released into the water, where they eventually combine to form a free-swimming planktonic larval stage. It all makes the Woodstock Festival and James Bond look amateur.

Northern Beaches

23km (14 miles) north of Cairns
North of Cairns, muddy mangrove swamps give way to the pretty Northern Beaches, home to the city's most affluent. It is here you will find the resorts of Palm Cove and Trinity Beach, both of which offer an attractive alternative base outside the city. The area is home to two high-profile attractions:

Skyrail Rainforest Cableway

The award-winning cableway gives visitors the unique opportunity to glide quietly over 7km (4¹⁄₃ miles) of pristine rainforest canopy and through the heart of the World Heritage-listed **Barron Gorge National Park** to the rainforest village of Kuranda. Although once a highly controversial project, it is now considered a global ecotourism success encompassing both education and great fun. The journey includes two stops: one to take in the views from Red Peak Station (545m/1,788ft), and another at Barron Falls Station where you can look around the entertaining Rainforest Interpretive Centre, the Barron River Gorge and the Barron Falls. Sadly, from April to December, the falls are little more than a trickle and only take on their postcard appearance during the wet season. From the Barron Falls Station you then cross the Barron River before arriving at Kuranda.

It's a good trip in any weather and is perhaps best combined with a day-tour package to Kuranda via the Kuranda Scenic Railway (*see opposite*).
Captain Cook Highway.
Tel: (07) 4038 1555. www.skyrail.com.au.
Open: 8.15am–5.15pm. Admission charge.

Tjapukai

Next door to the Skyrail terminal (coast side) is Tjapukai (pronounced 'Jaboguy'), an award-winning Aboriginal Cultural Park considered one of the best of its kind in Australia. It offers an entertaining and educational insight into the tribe's mythology, customs and history, as well as effective instruction in boomerang-throwing and didgeridoo-playing. The 'Tjapukai by Night' experience offers an interactive, traditional and dramatic 'corroboree' ritual and stage performance, followed by a buffet of regional food.

A mass of colourful wings from the millions of butterflies killed by vehicles in Queensland, but life abounds at the Butterfly Sanctuary, Kuranda

Captain Cook Highway.
Tel: (07) 4042 9900. www.tjapukai.com.au.
Open: 9am–5pm. Admission charge.

Kuranda

25km (15½ miles) north of Cairns
The pretty rainforest village of
Kuranda is the principal attraction
in the Atherton Tablelands. Its main
attractions are the **Heritage Market**
and **Original Market** that together
offer a vast range of souvenir-based art
and crafts (*Open: 9am–3pm*). Much of
it is kitsch, but there is some quality
work on offer at affordable prices.

Other attractions include the **Koala
Gardens** with the usual photo
opportunities (*Tel: (07) 4093 9953*);
Birdworld (*Tel: (07) 4093 9188.
www.birdworldkuranda.com*); and the
impressive **Australian Butterfly
Sanctuary** (*Tel: (07) 4093 7575.
www.australianbutterflies.com. Open:
daily 10am–4pm. Admission charge*).
The latter is reputedly the world's
largest and houses around a dozen
species, including the stunning Ulysses
Blue. A bright red or white hat is
recommended to attract the insects.

A few kilometres east of Kuranda
is the **Rainforestation Nature
Park** offering yet another chance
to experience Aboriginal culture
and see captive native animals
(*Kennedy Highway. Tel: (07) 4085 5008.
www.rainforest.com.au. Open: daily
10am–4pm. Admission charge*).

Kuranda Scenic Railway

Kuranda is best reached by either the
Skyrail (*see opposite*) or the Kuranda
Scenic Railway (or a combination
thereof). The railway negotiates the
Barron Gorge to Cairns, stopping at
viewpoints including the Barron Falls
along the way.
*Tel: (07) 4036 9333. www.ksr.com.au.
Departs Cairns: 8.30am & 9.30am
(except Sat). Departs Kuranda: 2pm
& 3.30pm. Admission charge.*

Cairns and the far north

A Skyrail gondola glides gently over the rainforest canopy on its way to Kuranda

Drive: The Atherton Tablelands

This drive ascends to the cooler climes of the Atherton Tablelands. Amid its green, lush landscapes are lakes and waterfalls, wildlife-rich national parks and historic settlements.

Information on the region can be found at **North Queensland Gateway Discovery Centre** *in Cairns (see p111), or* **Atherton Tableland Information Centre** *(Main St, Atherton. Tel: (07) 4091 4222. www.athertonsc.qld.gov.au).*

Allow at least a whole day for this 280km (174-mile) drive.

From Cairns head back south on the Bruce Highway to Gordonvale (24km/ 15 miles). At Gordonvale, head west on Gilles Rd following signs to Atherton.

Once on the plateau and about 10km (6km) before Yungaburra, take a short diversion north (right) on Boar Pocket Rd to the Cathedral Fig.

1 Danbulla Forest and Lake Tinaroo

Impressive Lake Tinaroo is popular for barramundi fishing. The Danbulla Forest that fringes its northern bank is bisected by 28km (17 miles) of unsealed scenic road that offers a few highlights. The **Cathedral Fig** (signposted off Gilles Rd) is a superb example of the strangler fig species. It is about 500 years old, over 50m (164ft) tall and 40m (131ft) around the base. The short diversion to the Haynes lookout (left off Boar Pocket Rd) is also worthy of investigation.
Return to Gilles Rd and continue to Yungaburra, stopping for a quick look (and refreshments) at Lake Barrine.

2 Yungaburra

One of the prettiest and most historic of the Tablelands settlements, with markets on the last Saturday of the month, this village is a great overnight stop, and you can attempt to spot wild platypus at dusk or dawn. A viewing platform is located at Petersen Creek. The **Curtain Fig** (*south, signposted off Atherton Rd*) is another fine example of the species.
Return to Atherton Rd and continue west to Atherton.

3 Atherton

Founded in part by Chinese gold prospectors in the late 1880s, Atherton is the largest town on the Tablelands. The restored **Hou Wang Temple** is one of very few Chinese remnants (*86 Herberton Rd. Tel: (07) 4091 6945.*

Open: 10am–4pm. Admission charge). Also popular is the 44km (27-mile) scenic **steam train trip to Herberton** aboard a restored 1920s C17 called 'Roger' (*Tel: (07) 4091 4222*). **Hasties Swamp**, 5km (3 miles) south of the town, offers remarkably diverse birdlife. *From Herberton Rd head east to Kennedy Highway (just south of Hasties Swamp) and continue south on Kennedy Highway.*

4 Mount Hypipamee National Park

This small pocket of dense rainforest has a volcanic crater lake, waterfalls and some very special wildlife, including 13 species of nocturnal possum and the Lumholtz's tree kangaroo. A short walk from the car park lies the ominous and impressive 95,000-year-old Crater Lake. *From the park head south, then east to Millaa Millaa township.*

5 The Waterfalls

Millaa Millaa Falls, **Zillie Falls** and **Ellinjaa Falls** can be explored on a 16km (10-mile) circuit, signposted just east of the town on the Palmerston Highway. Don't miss the **Millaa Millaa lookout** just to the west of Millaa Millaa (*Evelyn Rd*). At 850m (2,788ft), it offers spectacular views of the Bellenden Ker Range and the highest peak in Queensland, Mount Bartle Frere. *From Millaa Millaa drop back down to the coast via the Palmerston Highway (70km/43 miles). At Bruce Highway head back north to Cairns (88km/55 miles).*

Drive: The Atherton Tablelands

Port Douglas

70km (43 miles) north of Cairns

With its boutique shops, fine restaurants and upmarket accommodation, the small and classy coastal resort of Port Douglas offers a great alternative to the hype and commercialism of its larger counterpart. It is also a fine base from which to explore the Mossman Gorge, Daintree and Cape Tribulation, as well as the Great Barrier Reef, with numerous cruise options and activities on offer from the marina's **Mirage Complex** on Wharf St.

Visit the **Port Douglas Tourist Information Centre** for more details (*23 Macrossan St. Tel: (07) 4099 5599 & 1300 687 846. www.portdouglas.com.au. Open: 8.30am–5pm*).

The colourful weekly crafts market at Port Douglas

CRUISING AND DIVING ON THE BARRIER REEF

The number and variety of reef cruises and dive options can seem overwhelming in Queensland, particularly in Cairns, where all manner of vessels from skiffs to deluxe catamarans are chasing your tourist dollar. Some offer half-day island visits with snorkelling, while others offer introductory dives, multi-day dive courses or sail-dive combos. Most give you the opportunity to dive, even for the first time, with a minimum of training, or at the very least to don a mask, snorkel and goggles and enter the remarkable world beneath the waves. The most popular half-day trips with snorkelling are to Green or Fitzroy Islands or to the 'outer reef'. The 'outer islands' and 'outer reef' offer the best water clarity and the larger fish species and are recommended even for an introductory dive.

Four Mile Beach

On the southern flank of the peninsula, the beach attracts a cosmopolitan crowd and has a net to ward off box jellyfish and other stingers. Before picking your spot on the sand, check out the view of the beach from Flagstaff Hill (*turn right at the bottom of Macrossan St, then follow Wharf St onto Island Point Rd*). Anzac Park at the end of Macrossan St hosts a colourful market every Sunday.

Rainforest Habitat

The Rainforest Habitat offers a fine introduction to the region's rich flora and fauna, displaying over 180 species housed in three main habitat enclosures: 'wetlands', 'rainforest' and 'grassland'. The park also offers an interesting 'Breakfast with the Birds'

Cool off at Mossman Gorge

(8–11am) and 'Lunch with the Lorikeets' *(noon–2pm)*, both unique dining experiences.

6km (3¾ miles) from the centre of town, at the junction of Captain Cook Highway & Port Douglas Rd. Tel: (07) 4099 3235. www.rainforesthabitat.com.au. Open: 8am–5.30pm. Admission charge.

Mossman Gorge

The Mossman River, which bisects the vast **Daintree National Park**, is one of the principal watersheds for one of the most diverse and ancient rainforests on the planet. The small gorge 5km (3 miles) west of Mossman village offers a great place for a cooling dip, with a series of short walks following the river upstream to some fine swimming holes. While lazing in the pools you may be lucky enough to see either a Ulysses Blue or Cairns Birdwing butterfly. They are just two of some truly stunning species found in the park, with the former being the marketing moniker for the Wet Tropics region.

For more information contact the **QPWS office** in Mossman (*1 Front St. Tel: (07) 4098 2188. www.epa.qld.gov.au*).

A warning sign on the Daintree River

Daintree

113km (70 miles) north of Cairns
The former logging settlement of
Daintree sits at the fringes of the largely
impenetrable Daintree National Park
and on the banks of the Daintree River,
famed for its resident 'salties'
(crocodiles). Visitors can embark on
various leisurely cruises from the village
to the coast several times a day in
search of these ancient, ominous-
looking reptiles. You can either pick up
the cruise near the village or at various
points south to the Daintree-Cape
Tribulation ferry crossing. For bookings
call in at the information centre
(*5 Stewart St. Tel: (07) 4098 6120.
www.daintree village.asn.au*).

Daintree is also noted for its **Ecolodge
and Spa**, recognised as one of the best in
the world (*20 Daintree Rd. Tel: (07) 4098
6100. www.daintree-ecolodge.com.au*).
A wide-ranging menu of massages,

unique Aboriginal techniques, natural
ingredients and invigorating body
treatments are available to both
residents and day visitors.

Cape Tribulation

150km (93 miles) north of Cairns
Cape Tribulation is the name attributed
to a small settlement and headland that
forms the main tourist focus of the
area. However, the term is also loosely
used to describe the entire 40km
(25-mile) stretch of coastline within
the Daintree National Park from the
Daintree River mouth to the start of
the Bloomfield Track north of the
Cape. The ubiquitous Captain Cook
bestowed the name Tribulation upon it
in 1770 after his disastrous grounding
of the *Endeavour* just offshore.

This remarkable region is where
'rainforest meets reef' and visitors come
to this remote and protected wilderness

not only to witness the rich flora and fauna, but also to escape the commercialism and development of the major resort towns.

The Daintree River has also acted as a barrier to development and a short ferry crossing is required to access the area. It is about a 40-minute drive from the crossing to the Cape. About 6km (3³/4 miles) beyond the crossing (then east and signposted off Cape Tribulation Rd) is the **Daintree Discovery Centre** with its range of displays offering a fine introduction to the rich and unique biodiversity of the lush rainforest (*Tel: (07) 4098 9171. www.daintree-rec.com.au. Open: 8.30am–5pm. Admission charge*). An added attraction is a 400m (1,310ft) boardwalk and a 25m (82ft) tower offering a bird's-eye view of the forest canopy below. There is also a café.

Back on Cape Tribulation Rd and 9km (5¹/2 miles) before the settlement itself, look out for the **Marrdja Boardwalk**. Winding its way through the tidal mangrove, it is well worth a look and takes about 45 minutes. The shorter 1.2km (³/4-mile) **Dubuji Boardwalk** near Cape Tribulation is another option and equally good.

There are two fine beaches either side of the Cape and it is fringing these that you will find most of the accommodation options and the settlement's limited amenities. The Kulki picnic area and lookout is at the southern end of **Emmagen Beach** and is signposted just beyond the village. Just beyond that, the Kulki turn-off is the start of the **Mount Sorrow** track, a challenging 3.5km (2-mile) ascent with spectacular views from the 650m (2,130ft) summit. Again, you can guess who christened it!

Beyond Cape Tribulation the road gradually degenerates to form the notorious **Bloomfield Track** to Cooktown. From here you are entering real 'Croc Country' and a 4WD is essential.

The view from the start of the Bloomfield Track, Cape Tribulation

Captain Cook and the trials of Cape Tribulation

With names like Cape Tribulation, Mount Sorrow, Mount Misery and Darkie's Downfall, you get the distinct impression that James Cook was not a happy explorer in the far north of Queensland. Indeed, he was not.

The year was 1770 and the then 'Master' James Cook was on his first 'voyage of discovery' on board the *Endeavour* (1768–71). He had been hired by the Royal Society of London (formed in 1660) to observe the transit of Venus across the sun. These precise measurements were necessary to accurately determine longitude and therefore create accurate maps. Cook sailed from England in 1768 and in April 1769 had already made his observations of the transition off Tahiti and mapped the entire coastline of New Zealand. After sailing across the Tasman Sea his party then landed at Botany Bay on the eastern coast of Australia, the first recorded Europeans to do so. The date was 19 April 1770.

For the next two months Cook sailed north, mapping the East Coast before encountering the Great Barrier Reef just beyond Fraser Island. Given the size and construction of the vessels of the day, it was testament to Cook's remarkable navigational skills that he had not encountered disaster far sooner than northern Queensland. At the time, the closest thing to sonar was rope and a keen eye aided at night by oil lamps. So it was perhaps with some inevitability that the *Endeavour* ran aground on the night of 11 June. Holed and taking on water, the crew cleverly used a sail wrapped under the entire hull to stop the ship from sinking and with some

Statue of Captain James Cook, arguably the greatest explorer of all time, in Hyde Park, Sydney

An old map showing voyages from the Cook era

good fortune the tide did the rest.

Very carefully, Cook and his crew sailed the badly damaged vessel to safe harbour at what is now the Endeavour River. For seven weeks they made repairs and in so doing set up what was the first European settlement in Australia: Cooktown. Whilst in the region, the ship's botanist Joseph Banks recorded many new species to add to the 80-odd he had already recorded along the coast, including the genera 'Eucalyptus and Banksia'.

Once repairs were complete, Cook gingerly renegotiated the reef and after sailing through the Torres Strait, on 22 August he landed on Possession Island, where he claimed the entire coastline as British territory.

He returned to England via the Cape of Good Hope and St Helena, arriving back in his beloved homeland on 12 July 1771.

It was not until after his second voyage in search of the mythical *Terra australis* (1772–5) that Cook was promoted to captain, the title for which he is now best known.

He was an extraordinary man who rose from humble beginnings, and is widely regarded as the greatest explorer of all time. Tragically, despite his abiding respect for all the native peoples he encountered throughout his life, he was killed during a rare altercation with native Hawaiians in February 1779. He was aged 51.

Cooktown

334km (207 miles) from Cairns

No prizes for guessing who put this place on the map!

When the *Endeavour* ran aground on the reef in 1770, Captain Cook used what is now the Endeavour River and its shores for safe harbour and to carry out essential repairs. He spent two months here and in so doing effectively created the first white settlement in Australia. With Cook's departure, it lay dormant until the 1870s gold rush revitalised the settlement with, remarkably, around 30,000 hopeful souls taking up temporary residence. With the rush over, the town diminished, but today, with a population of around 2,000, it retains its proud connection with Cook and acts as the gateway to Cape York.

The **Visitor Information Centre** is located in the Botanical Gardens (*Finch Bay Rd. Tel: 1800 174 895 & (07) 4069 6004. www.cooktowns.com*).

Grassy Hill Lighthouse

With its extensive coastal views, this was the spot where Captain Cook reputedly worked out his safe passage back through the reef to the open sea. The old lighthouse was built in England and shipped to Cooktown in 1885. It was automated in 1927 and became obsolete in the 1980s.

End of Hope St, north of the town centre. Free access to viewing platform.

James Cook Museum

Housed in a former convent built in 1889 – just one of many historical

buildings in the town – the James Cook Museum makes a fine job of showcasing the town's pivotal association with the great man, and is the undeniable highlight here. Striking exhibits in the Endeavour Gallery include the ship's anchor and one of her cannons, supplemented with references to Cook's journals and oral tales from the local Aboriginals. Other features of the town's colourful and cosmopolitan past are included, with the Palmer River gold rush and two devastating cyclones being of particular interest.

Corner of Furneaux St & Helen St. Tel: (07) 4069 5386. Open: 9.30am–4pm (Apr–Jan); reduced hours (Feb–Mar), call for details. Admission charge.

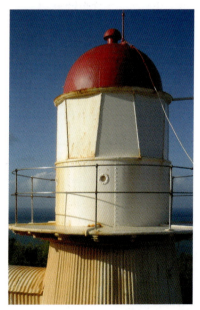

The Grassy Hill Lighthouse stands in a beautiful spot above Cooktown

The James Cook Museum is the highlight of Cooktown

Nature's Powerhouse

Also worth visiting is Nature's Powerhouse, an 'environment interpretive centre' in the Botanical Gardens. It boasts an impressive collection of botanical illustrations by lauded local artist Vera Scarth-Johnson. *Tel: (07) 4069 6004. www.naturespowerhouse.info. Open: daily 9am–5pm. Admission charge.*

Cape York

Beyond Cooktown, the great wilderness of Cape York beckons to the adventurous and the 4WD enthusiast. The 1,000km (620-mile) journey, much of which is unsealed road, takes at least 10–14 days return and is not for the faint-hearted. You have several options to reach the tip, including air charters and limited supply vessels from Cairns, but most go by road. Many embark on organised 4WD guided trips, while others undertake the trip independently, with all the detailed planning that an archetypal Australian adventure demands. A reliable vehicle, proper equipment and a dogged sense of adventure are all essential and the journey must be made in the dry season (Apr–Oct), when the numerous riverbed crossings are negotiable. Other than the exhilaration of reaching the northernmost tip of the continent, highlights along the way include the **Split Rock Aboriginal paintings** near Laura (*Tel: (07) 4060 3457. www.quikancc.com.au*) and the **Lakefield National Park**, the state's second-largest (*www.epa.qld.gov.au*).

Beyond Cooktown there is obviously a dearth of amenities and when it comes to accommodation there is little choice beyond basic roadhouses and campsites, and hotel pubs. The information centre in Cairns (*see pp110–11*) can supply up-to-date information about the Cape as well as organised trips.

Getting away from it all

Given the sheer size of Australia and the fact that the vast majority of its people (around 85 per cent) live in cities or coastal towns, it is not difficult to lose the crowds. You could just buy a map, pick a road – any road – and follow your nose. As long as you go prepared, Australia has much to offer travellers doing just that. But for most, with the inevitable time constraints, it is a case of sticking to a tight agenda.

By far the best 'get away' venues are the nation's remarkable national parks. New South Wales alone has about 600, ranging in size from a few hectares to 'a small African nation', with most on or within easy reach of the coast.

Sheer sandstone cliffs are typical of the Blue Mountains National Park

Another great option is the East Coast's myriad islands. There are over 900 along the Great Barrier Reef alone.

COASTAL NATIONAL PARKS

The following are just a sample of the best coastal national parks from Sydney to Cairns, but this is by no means a comprehensive list. For detailed information in New South Wales, refer to the **NPWS** (*National Parks and Wildlife Service. www.nationalparks.nsw.gov.au*), and in Queensland, the **QPWS** (*Queensland Parks and Wildlife Service. www.epa.qld.gov.au*).

New South Wales
Barrington Tops NP
74,568ha (184,260 acres)
Volcanic plateau rising to 1,500m (4,920ft). Varied habitat from subtropical to subalpine, waterfalls, rivers and short walks. Good escape from the coastal heat. Services and accommodation plentiful. Camping available.

Access/nearest town: Gloucester (34km/21 miles).

Blue Mountains NP
267,934ha (662,080 acres)
One of the largest and most popular in the state (*see pp44–5*). Sandstone escarpment and dense eucalyptus forest with spectacular viewpoints, waterfalls and 140km (87 miles) of walking tracks. Don't miss **Wentworth Falls**, **The Three Sisters** and **Govett's Leap**. Services and accommodation plentiful. Camping available.
Nearest town: Katoomba (in the heart of the national park).

Bundjalung NP
20,359ha (50,308 acres)
Over 38km (24 miles) of protected beach, lagoons, estuary and small pockets of lush rainforest (*see p60*). Don't miss the Iluka rainforest walk. Services and accommodation in Iluka. Excellent motor park and campsite at **Woody Head** (*Tel: (02) 6646 6134*).
Access via Iluka Rd (60km/37 miles north of Grafton off the Pacific Highway).

Dorrigo NP
11,902ha (29,410 acres)
World Heritage rainforest escarpment rising to over 1,000m (3,280ft) with many fine and easily accessible short walks (*see p57*). Don't miss the QPWS Rainforest Centre with its rainforest canopy 'Skywalk'. Services and accommodation plentiful. Camping available.

Access/nearest town: Dorrigo (2km/ 1¼ miles), or Bellingen (28km/17 miles).

Hat Head NP
7,459ha (18,520 acres)
Beach backed by coastal heath and large dune systems (*see p55*). Dramatic headlands, renowned for wildflowers, picturesque **Smoky Cape Lighthouse** and **Trail Bay Goal**. Services and accommodation plentiful, including former lighthouse-keepers' cottages. Camping available.
Access/nearest town: South West Rocks (3km/2 miles).

Mt Warning NP
2,455ha (6,066 acres)
Rainforest within the vast caldera (crater) and surrounding the remnant plug of an ancient volcano. The highlight is the climb to the 1,157m (3,795ft) peak at dawn. Services and accommodation plentiful. Camping available.
Access/nearest town: Murwillumbah (20km/12 miles).

Myall Lakes NP
47,594ha (117,607 acres)
Coastal lake system and 40km (25 miles) of beautiful beaches and headlands (*see pp50–51*). Also home to some of the tallest gum trees in the state (70m/229ft). Don't miss **Seal Rocks**. Services and accommodation plentiful. Camping available.
Access/nearest towns: (south) Bulahdelah (8km/5 miles) and (north) Forster/ Tuncurry (35km/22 miles).

New England NP

67,303ha (166,309 acres)

Similar but more remote and larger than Dorrigo NP. Don't miss Point Lookout with its stunning views and short bush walks (*see p57*). Good escape from the coastal heat. Accommodation and camping available (*Tel: (02) 6657 2309*).

Access/nearest towns: (east) Dorrigo (70km/43 miles), or (west) Armidale (85km/53 miles).

Queensland
Cape Hillsborough NP

816ha (2,016 acres)

A small park with a fine mix of beach and rocky headlands together with hoop-pine bush networked by short walks (*see p99*). Highlights include tame kangaroos. Excellent accommodation, motor park and campsite at the **Cape Hillsborough Nature Resort** (*see p169*).

Access/nearest town: Mackay (50km/ 31 miles).

Daintree NP

17,000ha (42,000 acres)

A World Heritage Site and one of the most biologically diverse areas in the world, comprising almost impenetrable ranges, river valleys and ancient tropical rainforests sweeping down to the coast (*see p119*). Don't miss a cool dip at Mossman Gorge. Excellent range of accommodation in and around Daintree and Cape Tribulation. Limited camping.

Limited access via Mossman, Daintree and Cape Tribulation. Cairns is 104km (65 miles) south.

Eungella NP

51,700ha (127,755 acres)

Elevated tropical rainforest and one of Queensland's most ecologically diverse parks (*see p99*). There are 860 plant species alone and a wonderful variety of wildlife with platypus seen regularly. Good short walks. Limited services and accommodation. Camping available.

Access/nearest town: Mackay (80km/ 50 miles).

Great Sandy NP (Cooloola)

16,370ha (40,450 acres)

The mainland Cooloola section of the park is a protected remote beach backed by sand dunes, heaths, freshwater lakes and forests (*see p90*). Highlights include ancient coloured

Licuala palms dominate the bush near Mission Beach

sand cliffs and canoe adventures on the Noosa River in the southern section of the park. Services and accommodation are plentiful. Camping available.
Access into the park by 4WD only. Nearest towns: (south) Tewantin/Noosa (8km/5 miles) and (north) Rainbow Beach (2km/1¼ mile).

Lamington and Springbrook NPs
24,015ha (59,342 acres)
Known as the 'Green Behind the Gold', these two magnificent World Heritage-listed parks are home to a remarkable subtropical rainforest biodiversity that clings to the rim of the vast Mt Warning caldera (*see pp70–71*). Highlights include waterfalls, superb rainforest walks and dramatic viewpoints. Limited services and accommodation in the park. Camping available.
Access/nearest town: (Lamington) Canungra (40km/25 miles) and (Springbrook) Nerang (42km/26 miles).

'OUTBACK' NATIONAL PARKS
Although it will take some time to get there, a journey to one of the inland ('outback') national parks can be very rewarding and offers a stark contrast to the coast. For some, the outback, with its endless horizons and oceanic skies, is what Australia is all about.

Carnarvon NP
16,000ha (39,540 acres)
Carnarvon Gorge is one of Queensland's most visited outback parks and one of its most aesthetically and geologically

WHERE TO SEE WILDLIFE ON THE EAST COAST

Apart from the numerous East Coast wildlife sanctuaries, the following areas are recommended for 'wild encounters':
Dolphins: Tin Can Bay, Cooloola (QLD) and Tangalooma Dolphin Resort, Moreton Island (QLD).
Dugong: Hinchinbrook Island (QLD).
Echidnas: Common in both rural and urban environments.
Fairy penguins: As far north as Coffs Harbour (NSW), occasionally even in Sydney Harbour.
Flying foxes: Botanical Gardens, Sydney, and in Bellingen (NSW).
Kangaroos: Just about anywhere in open country, especially early or late in the day.
Koalas: Port Macquarie (NSW) and Magnetic Island (QLD).
Platypus: Eungella National Park and Yungaburra, Atherton Tablelands (QLD).
Saltwater crocodiles: Daintree and Cape York (QLD).
Turtles: Mon Repos, Bundaberg and Heron Island (QLD).
Whales: Hervey Bay (QLD), occasionally in and around Sydney Harbour.
Wombats: Common in both NSW and QLD.

dramatic. Towering sandstone cliffs and gorges host a diverse flora and fauna and some of the best examples of Aboriginal rock art in the country. Resort and lodge accommodation and camping.
Access 44km (27 miles) off Carnarvon Highway. Nearest towns: (south) Roma (180km/112 miles) and (north) Emerald (191km/119 miles).

Undara Volcanic NP
17,600ha (43,490 acres)
This park contains one of the planet's longest lava tube cave systems. Around

190,000 years ago, during a violent volcanic eruption and subsequent lava flow, the top, outer layer cooled and formed a crust, while the molten lava below drained outwards, leaving behind a series of hollow tubes, now home to many species of plants and animals. **Undara Experience Lava Lodge**, located adjacent to the park, offers a wide variety of accommodation, facilities, guided tours and activities (*Tel: (07) 4097 1900. www.undara.com.au*).
Access 330km (205 miles) south of Cairns.

BARRIER REEF ISLANDS

Considered the greatest natural attraction in the country and one of the best in the world, there is no disputing the aesthetic appeal of the Great Barrier

Mission Beach with Dunk Island in the distance

Reef both above and below the waves, or indeed the vast range of activities on offer to experience it fully. But with over 2 million visitors a year, is it possible to escape the crowds? Well, thanks to the sheer size and diversity of the reef, you can, and one of the best ways to do so is to visit one of its many islands. The reef has over 900 and – surprisingly – only 23 cater for tourists, with the remainder fully protected against wholesale development. Some, like Hinchinbrook, are very large and offer little in the way of amenities beyond basic campsites with a long-drop (toilet), while others, such as Hayman, are small and have luxury resorts.

The following are just a sample of the best on offer and omit those islands (including Hinchinbrook, Great Keppel, Whitsundays, Magnetic and Dunk), which are already detailed in the main text.

For more information on all islands contact the nearest regional visitor information centre and their associated websites or the **Queensland Parks and Wildlife Servic**e (*www.epa.qld.gov.au*).

Southern Reef (Bundaberg to Rockhampton)
Heron Island
18ha (44 acres), 72km (45 miles) northeast of Gladstone
Coral cay and part national park, with fringing platform reef supporting around 900 of the 1,500 fish species and 72 per cent of the coral species

found on the Great Barrier Reef.
Hugely popular diving spot. Full
resort facilities (*Tel: 1300 134 044.
www.heronisland.com*).
Access by sea or air from Gladstone.

Lady Elliot Island
*40ha (100 acres), 85km (53 miles)
northeast of Bundaberg*
A coral cay considered the first island of
the Barrier Reef. Activities on the island
include turtle- and whale-watching.
Renowned for its water clarity and
resident population of manta rays.
A small eco-oriented resort provides
accommodation from suites to tent
cabins (*Tel: 1800 072 200.
www.ladyelliot.com.au*).
*Access by air from Gladstone, Bundaberg,
Hervey Bay, Maroochydore, Brisbane
and the Gold Coast.*

Lady Musgrave Island
*14ha (34 acres), 105km (65 miles) north
of Bundaberg*
A small, uninhabited coral cay with
1,192ha (2,945 acres) of surrounding
reef, the island is a national park.
Camping available with transfers
from Town of 1770. No amenities,
including water.
*Access by day-cruise from Town of 1770
or from Bundaberg by seaplane.*

Northern Reef
(Townsville to Cooktown)
Fitzroy Island
*339ha (838 acres), 22km (14 miles)
southeast of Cairns*

Continental island with the vast
majority of it a national park.
Renowned for its walking tracks,
lookouts, beaches and snorkelling.
Mid-range resort with full amenities
and range of accommodation.
Camping available (*Tel: (07) 4051 9588.
www.huntgroup.com.au*). Day visitors
welcome.
Access by boat from Cairns.

Lizard Island
*1,000ha (2,470 acres), 93km (58 miles)
northwest of Cooktown*
Continental island group close to
the outer reef and arguably the best
accessible island on the entire reef.
Exquisite mix of natural beauty and
activities, with diving a speciality. One
quality upmarket resort (*Tel: 1300 134
044. www.lizardisland.com.au*) and basic
QPWS camping facilities (*contact
QPWS for details*).
*Access by air and boat from Cairns, Port
Douglas and Cooktown.*

Orpheus Island
*1,368ha (3,380 acres), 80km (50 miles)
north of Townsville*
Large continental island national park
with eight sandy beaches and some of
the best island coral beds on the reef.
Single exclusive resort (42 guests
maximum) offering luxurious
amenities and a wide range of self-
guided or organised activities
(*Tel: (07) 4777 7377.
www.orpheus.com.au*).
Access by air from Townsville or Cairns.

When to go

Given the length and geographical position of Australia's East Coast, some of its appeal is that at any time of year there is always a part of it that offers the ideal outdoor climate. Sydney is one of the most happening cities on earth and so plays a leading role in any visit, but it is supported admirably by such high-profile tourist centres as Byron Bay, the Gold Coast and Cairns, where there is plenty going on all year round, from festivals to local markets.

Climate and weather

Chances are, you are not coming to Australia's eastern seaboard to dance in the rain, snowboard, or snuggle up by an open fire (although you can do all three) and are instead intent on hitting the beach armed with little except your best polka-dot bikini, first pair of surf shorts, shades and sun block.

Naturally, you are just about guaranteed lots of sun and those 'ooh, now that is perfect' temperatures, but Australia can actually surprise you with some pretty dramatic weather – and at any time of year. The East Coast can see some wild weather events, including damaging storms (particularly in summer), floods and even cyclones in the north.

Of course, being a southern hemisphere continent, Australia's seasons are the opposite of those in the northern hemisphere and this is usually part of the attraction. Broadly speaking, the peak summer season between Sydney and Brisbane is from the middle of November through to the end of February. Temperatures at this time are generally in the mid 20s°C to low 30s°C (high 70s°F to high 80s°F) and clear sunny days the norm. Conversely, however, these same months are considered the low season north of Rockhampton (Tropic of Capricorn), when the wet season brings almost unbearably hot and humid conditions. Climate aside, this is also 'stinger season' in the far north, which presents

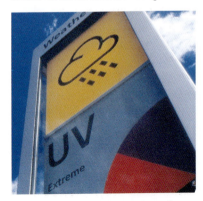

It's not always sunny on the East Coast of Australia

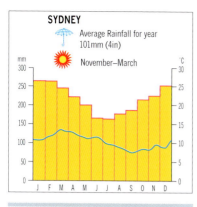

SYDNEY

Average Rainfall for year
101mm (4in)

November–March

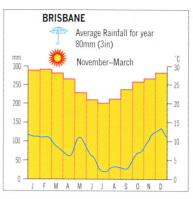

BRISBANE

Average Rainfall for year
80mm (3in)

November–March

WEATHER CONVERSION CHART

25.4mm = 1 inch

°F = 1.8 × °C + 32

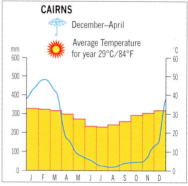

CAIRNS

December–April

Average Temperature
for year 29°C/84°F

its own dangers as the highly poisonous jellyfish come out to play.

If planning a long trip, say three months or more, try to make spring or autumn the core of your time.

Events, domestic and school holidays

Australia hosts many internationally significant events of all types and sizes, and the ongoing list of domestic and regional events is vast. From sport to fashion and from music to art there is always plenty happening, especially in the main centres of Sydney, the Gold Coast and Brisbane. You may be coming to Australia to attend a specific event or make your travels along the East Coast coincide with others, but one thing is guaranteed: particularly in summer, you will never be short of choice.

Australians are notorious for their enviable lifestyle, so bear in mind that when it comes to getting out there and enjoying yourself, the foreign visitor is often in the minority, especially in summer and school holidays. Between 24 December and February, you can forget the nine-to-five modus operandi. At this time, just about everybody heads to the beach, so book accommodation and activities well in advance.

Also be conscious of other school holidays, which happen a week or two around Easter, a couple of weeks in June and July and another couple of weeks during September and October.

Getting around

By far the best way to see the East Coast is independently, using a hired vehicle (usually a campervan), or for longer visits buying one second-hand. Of course, the latter does present its own dangers, but because so many people choose this option, Sydney and the main centres are well geared to sales both for seller or buyer and, with care, you can certainly secure a reliable bargain and sell it again before departure.

However, if time is short and you want to cover a lot of ground, you may have to be more specific about your itinerary, focus on only a few locations and then combine domestic air travel with short-term vehicle hire. This option is becoming increasingly popular given the very competitive prices of domestic flights currently available and car hire in the main centres. Public transport up and down the coast and within its main centres is based on a variety of air, bus, ferry and train networks, and is generally quite good, although in Sydney delays should be expected.

Public transport
By air
Sydney, Brisbane and Cairns all possess an international airport, and there are modern domestic airports at Coolangatta (for Gold Coast and Byron Bay), Hervey Bay (for Fraser Island), Rockhampton, Mackay and Townsville. There are three main domestic carriers

covering the East Coast route and vying for the tourist dollar, so prices are very competitive: **Qantas** (*Tel: 131 313. www.qantas.com.au*), **Virgin Blue** (*Tel: 136 789. www.virginblue.com.au*) and **Jetstar** (*Tel: 131 538. www.jetstar.com.au*). By far the best and cheapest way to book is well in advance and on the Internet. There are also several regional airways operating smaller planes on specialist routes. For up-to-date information contact your destination's tourist office.

By bus
The interstate bus services offer an easy way to move up and down the coast but, given the distances involved, it can prove uncomfortable. **Greyhound** (*Tel: 1300 473 946. www.greyhound.com.au*) and **Premiere Motor Services** (*Tel: 133 410. www.premierems.com.au*) are the main players. Their network follows all the main interstate highways up and down the coast, with offshoots

including the Blue Mountains, New England (Hunter Valley), Charters Towers, the Atherton Tablelands and so on. As well as scheduled routes and fares, they offer jump-on, jump-off passes.

There are many other smaller regional companies; for information contact the relevant visitor information centre. **Countrylink** (*see below*) also offers coach services to some centres in conjunction with rail schedules between New South Wales and Queensland.

By train

Given the price and convenience of domestic flights, train travel up and down the East Coast is usually the domain of the enthusiast, but it remains a viable mode of transport. One trip well worth considering is a jaunt into the outback from Rockhampton ('Spirit of the Outback'), or Cairns ('Savannahlander'). Both routes are operated by **Queensland Rail** (*Tel: 132 232. www.qr.com.au*). In New South Wales **Countrylink** (*Tel: 132 232.*

Sydney's Monorail glides through Darling Harbour

www.countrylink.nsw.gov.au) offers rail and rail/coach services state-wide. The line gauge differs from that of Queensland, so between the two states coach connections are provided from Brisbane for onward travel.

In Sydney and Brisbane metro train services are linked to bus and ferry networks and as such offer an excellent way of negotiating the city. In Sydney contact **CityRail** (*Tel: 131 500. www.cityrail.nsw.gov.au*), and in Brisbane **TransLink** (*Tel: 131 230. www.translink.com.au*).

Independent travel
Car or campervan?
Again, given the size of Australia, car hire is usually reserved for city and regional travel, with the long haul becoming the domain of the almost iconic campervan. In summer, the main highways up and down the coast are awash with them, and not just foreign

A campervan is a great way to explore the East Coast's many national parks visitors, but many Australians (especially retirees or 'Grey Nomads' as they are dubbed) have campervans, camper trailers (in essence a tent on wheels) and the ubiquitous 'Jayco' caravans.

If you live in a small, heavily populated country, travelling by vehicle in Australia will be an enlightening experience. Distances are huge and subsequent travelling times between the major cities, towns and sights will raise eyebrows. But instead of getting bored and fighting the odometer, relax and make driving part of the whole holiday experience.

If you are travelling for more than three months, consider buying a car or a van, or hiring a campervan. East Coast roads are generally in good condition and sealed, with only back roads (especially within the national parks) requiring 4WD. If you intend to do some off-road driving, see a bit of the outback, or want to investigate the national parks fully, you should hire a 4WD campervan, but it will obviously cost more. Fraser Island is 4WD only so if you plan a visit there, bear this in mind when deciding on a vehicle for your travels. However, always check with the hire company where you can and cannot take your 4WD vehicle (some will not allow them off graded roads or on sand, like Fraser Island). Also check your liability in the case of an accident.

There are numerous hire companies in Australia and you are advised to shop around for the best deal. Campervan models vary from the basic two-berth van to the travelling family palace starting from $60 a day. The main players are **Britz** (*Tel: 1800 331 454. www.britz.com*) and **Maui** (*Tel: 1300 363 800. www.maui-rentals.com*). Standard vehicles can be hired for around $50 a day in the main centres and all the major international firms are present. It is worth looking at smaller companies, however, as they often offer great deals, but as with any hire agreement always read the small print before signing a contract.

Fuel costs

Fuel costs are generally favourable in comparison to the UK or USA, but, like most places, they are rising rapidly. Be aware that unleaded can be up to 15 per cent more expensive outside the main cities. Diesel is currently more expensive than unleaded, but is less prone to price fluctuations. Given the distances, when it comes to budgeting you will find fuel expenses exceed those of food and rival those of accommodation. Allow at least 18 cents per kilometre for fuel alone. On long journeys follow the standard rules for minimizing costs: ensure correct tyre pressures, avoid using A/C if possible, check the oil regularly, stick to 90–100kph (56–62mph) and of course try to hunt out the cheapest fuel! A trip up and down the East Coast can easily involve driving 15,000+ km (9,300+miles). Choosing an economical vehicle and conserving fuel can save a lot of money.

Getting around

Accommodation

East Coast Australia offers a vast range of accommodation options to suit all budgets, from cheap national park campsites to exclusive and luxurious island resorts. Regardless of budget there is rarely a problem finding a clean, comfortable bed anywhere along the East Coast, but during high season you are advised to book all accommodation well in advance. The local visitor information centres can supply full listings and book on your behalf.

Given the climate, the cheap and cheerful camping option (outside the cities) can be very much part of the great Australian experience. Somehow, nothing beats being in a national park campsite under the stars, beside the open fire and within earshot of the surf, let alone in the company of several possums and a small squadron of kookaburras! Beyond island resorts and national parks, other unique options include the lighthouse-keepers' cottages at Smoky Cape (*see p55*), or several days under sail exploring the Whitsunday Islands (*see pp99–101*).

B&Bs, farmstays and self-catering

Rarely a budget option, most B&Bs are mid- to high-end, offering comfortable accommodation, usually en suite, often in historic houses or on farms. Hosts are usually friendly and informative and on farm properties you can normally muck in with the day-to-day activities. Some B&Bs are actually a semi or fully self-contained cottage or cabin with breakfast supplied. As well as private houses, caravan parks and hostels, some resorts and motels provide self-contained, self-catering options. Good websites include *www.bedandbreakfast.com.au* and *www.babs.com.au.com*

Camping

Most national parks allow camping in designated areas. Facilities tend to be minimal, with basic toilets, fireplaces and perhaps tank water; a few have barbecues and shower blocks. Payment is often by self-registration, and barbecues often require coins. If there are fireplaces you must bring your own wood. No fires may be lit, even stoves, during a Total Fire Ban. Even if water is supposedly available it is not guaranteed nor is it usually drinkable, so take a supply, as well as your own toilet paper. For camping details and bookings contact the **National Parks and Wildlife Service** (*www.nationalparks.nsw.gov.au*) and

A typical resort in the Whitsunday Islands

Queensland Parks and Wildlife Service (*www.epa.qld.gov.au*).

Caravan and tourist parks

Almost every town will have at least one caravan park with unpowered and powered sites for campers, caravans and campervans, an ablution block and usually a camp kitchen and/or barbecues. Most also offer self-contained villas and cabins. Check out **Big 4** (*Tel: 1800 632 444. www.big4.com.au*) and **Family Parks of Australia** (*Tel: 1800 682 492. www.familyparks.com.au*).

Hostels

There are many quality hostels in the main centres and all along the coast. Australia is also setting the pace with the new 'Flashpacker' concept, which in essence is a modern budget hotel with all the usual hostel facilities. Most offer double and twins (often with en suite) as well as singles and dorms. Kitchen and common-room facilities are generally good and many offer free breakfast and pick-up. The best hostel association is the **YHA** (*Tel: (02) 9261 1111. www.yha.org.au*).

Hotels, motels and resorts

In Sydney, Brisbane, the Gold Coast and Cairns there are plenty of high-end hotel options, with some, like Sydney's Hyatt, or the Gold Coast's Palazzo Versace, enjoying global recognition. Elsewhere, the islands are the reserve of many world-class hotels and resorts, especially on Fraser, the Whitsundays and the Great Barrier Reef, with some like Hayman or Lizard looking like something from a 007 movie set. In the main cities there are also many smaller boutique hotels and mid-range options. Some 'hotels', outside the major towns, are traditional pubs with basic motel-style rooms with shared facilities. Motels in Australia are usually depressingly anonymous, but dependably clean and comfortable.

Food and drink

For those that think Australian cuisine is throwing a shrimp on the 'barbie', they are in for a pleasant surprise. In many a sunny backyard nationwide, or at the beach, a sausage and the stalwart fish and chips still rule, but when it comes to fine dining it's a very different story. Given the increasingly cosmopolitan population and subsequently rich and varied cultural influences, Modern Australian 'fusion' cuisine is rapidly developing into something dynamic, unique and world-class.

Natural ingredients

Although Australia is the driest continent on earth, around its coastal fringes and along its major river watersheds it manages to produce a surprising abundance and variety of fruit and vegetables from the humble head of broccoli to the exotic mango. Australia exports staple grains like wheat, and produces many of its own dairy products. Beef and lamb are also home grown, as are some farmed native animals like kangaroo, emu and even crocodile. Of course, there is also plenty of seafood, with many species of warm-water fish like snapper, as well as some unusual crustaceans like Moreton Bay bugs and crayfish. Mussels, oysters and abalone are all also harvested locally. Native freshwater fish such as barramundi are popular as well as the more conventional and farmed species like trout.

Imported Asian ingredients are also commonly found in major cities because of the country's large Asian population and include the essentials like lemon grass, chilli and Thai basil. Markets are common, especially in rural areas, where fresh locally grown fare can be bought cheaply. Organic food is still something enjoyed and sought after by the minority, but, like most countries, this is changing along with growing concern about genetically modified (GM) foods.

Vegetarians are generally well catered for with some city restaurants concentrating on just that. Although you can find some excellent European-style cafés in the cities and major towns, the distinction between cafés, bistros and restaurants is becoming somewhat blurred. Unfortunately, like other Western countries, fast food is also a major feature and the infamous McDonald's and Starbucks-type brands are omnipresent.

Although it all sounds like a remarkable cornucopia, the country is not immune to the impact of drought and, of course, climate change. For almost three years it has suffered its worst drought on record and the effects are beginning to be felt in supply and cost right across the board.

Eating out

Thanks to the tourism appeal of the East Coast, restaurants are common even in smaller towns. Sydney and Melbourne are the undisputed gourmet capitals of Australia, though Brisbanites would dispute that. There is plenty of choice and, outside the high-profile city restaurants, you will find eating out generally cheaper than in Europe or the US. Most restaurants are licensed for the consumption of alcohol. Some are BYO (Bring Your Own), in which case you provide wine or beer and there is just a small corkage fee. Tipping is not mandatory, but the usual 10–15 per cent is appreciated by waiting staff.

Drink

Australian wine needs no introduction, being a major export and having made its mark on the world scene over the last two decades. The Hunter, Barossa and Yarra are words now synonymous with fine wine. In New South Wales, the Hunter Valley provides one of the best vineyard experiences in the world, with over 120 wineries, backed up by world-class accommodation, restaurants and wine-tasting tours.

Compared to Europe, Australian beer and lager leave a lot to be desired, but the climate is hardly conducive to supping creamy ale at room temperature. The big brands in New South Wales and Queensland are Tooheys (NSW) and Castlemaine XXXX (QLD). As well as being available on draught in pubs, beer is also available from bottleshops (or 'bottle-o's') in cases (or 'slabs') of cans ('tinnies' or 'tubes') or bottles ('stubbies'). This is by far the cheapest way of buying beer.

Sydney's famous Doyles Seafood Restaurant set beachside at Watsons Bay

Entertainment

Given its social history, Australia has earned a reputation as a cultural desert, but this has more to do with foreign arrogance than reality and, although it may hold some truth in remote rural areas, in the cities and major towns of modern Australia it is certainly not the case. Again, given the rich cosmopolitan make-up and subsequent cultural diversity of the nation, it certainly offers an entertainment culture on a par with any other and although (beyond the Aboriginal) it may lack some historical depth, there is no disputing the quality or diversity.

For up-to date listings refer to the local papers. In Sydney, see the *Sydney Morning Herald* (*www.smh.com.au*).

Film and theatre

With blockbusters like *Mad Max*, *Mission: Impossible* and *The Matrix* all being filmed in Australia, film and cinema is alive and well here. Most towns have at least one venue, with some offering outdoor screenings. You'll pay around $15 for an adult ticket and prices are usually reduced on Tuesdays.

Sydney and Brisbane have some excellent theatres, some of which are not only historic but of world standing. Although Australia is generally the last to see them, high-profile international shows and performances usually include Sydney on their tour agenda.

Starcity Casino, Pyrmont, Sydney

The national talent and resident theatrical company performances are also well worth investigating and annual festivals only enrich the modern repertoire.

Opera, music and dance

Sydney Opera House is the best-known operatic venue in the world and Opera Australia, based there, is the country's principal opera company. They offer around 600 performances a year, with an eight-month annual programme in Sydney. Performances are also staged in Melbourne and other regional centres (*for more information, tel: (02) 9318 8200; www.opera-australia.org.au*).

Classical music performances are also of the highest standard, as is contemporary dance, with one company – **Bangarra** – performing a unique fusion of Aboriginal and contemporary styles (*www.bangarra.com.au*).

Rock music abounds in pubs, and both national and high-profile international bands play Sydney and Brisbane on a regular basis.

Pubs, clubs and casinos

The nation's many hotels, pubs and nightclubs provide much of the country's nightlife and entertainment. Rural establishments tend to espouse the traditional Aussie hotel-cum-pub aesthetic, while city establishments go for the state-of-the-art, cocktail approach. As in many other countries, gimmicky pseudo-Irish pubs are

Earning extra pocket money on Circular Quay

common, but it is also possible to find a more authentic open-fire and real-ale establishment in Sydney.

Many establishments offer regular live music, DJs, karaoke, comedy and quiz nights, but it is perhaps gambling and the infamous 'pokies' (slot machines) that are the biggest draw, especially in rural areas. Australia is a nation of gamblers and as well as the ubiquitous slot machines, casinos are big business in Sydney, Brisbane and Cairns.

Nightclubs are generally only found in the cities and then usually only open towards the end of the week and at weekends. They charge an entry fee and attract the latest big-name DJs from around the world.

Shopping

With Sydney often placed alongside New York, Paris and London as one of the major world capitals, it certainly will not disappoint as a shopping destination. Be it clothing or anything else, the renowned labels and brands are all in evidence and are liberally supplemented with unique Australian products like opals or Aboriginal art. Many of the city's major shopping venues also add to the experience, being housed in stunning historical icons such as Sydney's Queen Victoria Building, built in 1898.

Local markets are a fine place to source unique, quality Australian-made products and you will find these in all the cities, major towns and tourist-oriented rural areas. Of course, tourist kitsch abounds and you will encounter many outlets pedalling koala backpacks and Steve Irwin (Crocodile Hunter) dolls. And as for the cork hat... don't even go there. It may stop the flies but these days you will never spot an Australian wearing one.

Aboriginal art and craft

Almost everyone is familiar with the unique and colourful dot-style Aboriginal art. In the tourist shops these designs are as ubiquitous as cuddly koalas, and printed on everything from didgeridoos to tea towels. Though beautiful, be aware that many have no link to Aboriginal people whatsoever and do not benefit them directly. The best thing to do is ask the dealer and check the label. Beyond specialist art dealers in the city, genuine Aboriginal art and

craft is more commonly available in country areas close to Aboriginal communities or from Aboriginal-owned or operated enterprises.

In Sydney, try the **Authentic Aboriginal Art Centre** (*45 Argyle St, The Rocks. Tel: (02) 9251 4474*) or the **Boomalli Aboriginal Artists**

Interior of the Queen Victoria Building, Sydney

Co-operative (*55–59 Flood St, Leichhardt. Tel: (02) 9560 2541. www.boomalli.org.au*). The local tourist information centres can also often point you in the right direction.

For authentic didgeridoos look no further than **Didj Beat Didgeridoo Shop** (*Clocktower Square Mall, The Rocks. Tel: (02) 9251 4289. www.didjbeat.com*).

Clothing and accessories
Beyond the designer fashion labels, iconic Australian clothing generally falls into the classic 'outback' stockman image, with Akubra hats (the Australian version of the US Stetson), leather ankle boots, moleskin trousers and oilskin (Driza-bone) rain jackets and capes the mainstay. For all these items look no further than the all-Australian company **RM Williams** (*389 George St & Shop 1–2 Chiefly Plaza, corner of Hunter St & Phillip St, Sydney. www.rmwilliams.com.au*). They have outlets or distributors in most major towns and, although pricey, the attire is of the best quality.

Australian surfwear is sought after world-wide and is a good buy. Look for labels such as Ripcurl, Quiksilver, Mambo and Billabong.

For Australian fashion, look out for names like Scanlan and Theodore, Country Road, Collette Dinnigan and Trent Nathan, while for wearable art try Weiss (black and white symbolic art often depicting native animals).

Colourful sarongs at the Eumundi Markets, near Noosa

Jewellery
With its rich geological resources, Australia offers a fine range of precious gems and quality jewellery. Opals are a speciality, but pearls and diamonds are also popular. The widest range is available in the cities, with some outlets in Sydney specialising solely in opals, such as **Opal Minded** (*36–64 George St. Tel: (02) 9247 9885*).

Markets
In Sydney the best markets are held every weekend in **The Rocks** (*Open: Sat & Sun*); **Paddington** (*395 Oxford St. Open: Sat*); **Glebe** (*Public School, Glebe Point Rd. Open: Sun*); and **Bondi** (*Campbell Parade. Open: Sun*). In Queensland don't miss the markets at **Eumundi** near Noosa (*see p88*) and **Kuranda** near Cairns (*see p115*).

Sport and leisure

Australians love their sport and for many it takes on an almost religious significance. Major national and international sporting events take place throughout the year and you should try to experience at least one high-profile event at a major arena such as the SCG (Sydney Cricket Ground) or The Gabba in Brisbane. When it comes to your participation and other outdoor pursuits and activities, the great Australian climate lends itself to a vast array of options, from ballooning to wreck-diving.

Participatory sports and activities

Australia is one of the world's great adventure and activity destinations, and, apart from those listed below, other well-served activities include canyoning and horse riding (Blue Mountains), cycling and mountain biking (Byron Bay), skydiving (Mission Beach and Byron Bay) and golf (Sydney and the Gold Coast).

Specialist tour operators offer many of the best experiences, and some pre-arrival research is recommended. The state, regional and local tourism websites listed throughout this guide are a good place to start.

Diving

There are many excellent dive sites all along the coast. In NSW the Solitary Islands off Coffs Harbour and Julian Rocks off Byron Bay are of particular note. Nothing, however, beats the Great Barrier Reef. Many combine their first diving experience with a basic course and, other than Cairns, the top locations for learning include Townsville and Magnetic Island. Visit *www.diveoz.com.au* and *www.scubaaustralia.com.au* for more information.

Looking for a good break at Coolangatta

Fishing

Thanks to the climate, and particularly the abundance of warm saltwater species, fishing is one of Australia's favourite pastimes. Sea-fishing charters are a feature of most coastal towns, while in the far north some operators also concentrate on freshwater species, including the legendary barramundi. See *www.fishnet.com.au* and *www.sportsfishaustralia.com.au*

Four-wheel-driving (4WD)

Fraser Island offers a truly world-class and easily accessible opportunity for off-roading. Especially if shared by a small group, hiring is affordable and can be combined with camping.

Sea kayaking and rafting

Sea kayaking is well worth considering anywhere along the east coast, with the Noosa River, Whitsunday and Barrier Reef Islands recommended. White-water rafting is also a feature in the far north of Queensland.

Surfing, windsurfing and kitesurfing

Due to the wave-taming influence of the Great Barrier Reef, surfing is generally confined to beaches south of Fraser Island. Sydney's many beaches are excellent, as are those of Newcastle, Port Macquarie and Byron Bay. In Queensland, Coolangatta is world-famous while Maroochydore and Noosa also have good breaks. Lessons are readily available in Sydney, Byron Bay and Noosa. Check out *www.surfinfo.com.au* and *www.realsurf.com* for details.

Windsurfing and kitesurfing are also widespread, with Noosa being a good place for the latter. See *www.windsurfing.org*

Spectator sports

Australian Rules Football

Also called 'Aussie rules' or just plain 'footy', to the uninitiated this winter sport is second only to cricket in being utterly baffling. Although most cities and states field teams, the true heartland is in Victoria. Matches can be seen at Sydney Cricket Ground and at The Gabba in Brisbane. Tickets can be purchased from Ticketek (*Tel: 132849; www.ticketek.com.au*).

Cricket

The national team defeats the rest of the world with almost tiring consistency. Cricket is a summer sport and the major venues on the east coast are the SCG (*www.sydneycricketground.com.au*) and The Gabba (*www.thegabba.org.au*).

Rugby

Both Rugby Union and Rugby League have a major following in Australia. The national team is known as the Wallabies and they have lifted the Rugby World Cup twice in 1991 and again in 1999. Rugby is a winter sport and regional and national games take place frequently in the main centres (*rugby.com.au; australianrugbyleague.com*).

Australia's sporting heroes

If America's answer to royalty or celebrity is the latest Hollywood A-lister, then in Australia it is the nation's sporting heroes. It would be rude not to start with that most popular of Australian sports – cricket – and arguably the greatest sportsman of them all, Sir Donald Bradman (1908–2001). 'The Don' (as he is known) had a glittering career spanning 21 years. He represented Australia in 52 Test matches, scoring 6,996 runs, and retired with a batting average of 99.94, nearly twice that of the next nearest Test batsman. He is also noted for one innings of 452 runs for NSW at the Sydney Cricket Ground. This record still stands unchallenged as the highest-ever first-class mark compiled in Australia. On his retirement, Bradman became the first Australian player to be knighted.

Living cricketing legends, now retired, include wicketkeeper Rodney Marsh (1947–) known as 'Iron Gloves'. Dennis Lillee (1949–) was the outstanding fast bowler of his time and claimed a world-record 355 Test wickets. Much slower in pace but no less devastating was Shane Warne (1969–), widely regarded as the world's finest leg spin bowler. His 708 wickets sits in second place for the most wickets taken in Test cricket. True to modern times, his career was plagued by scandals off the field, including a playing ban for testing positive for a prohibited substance, and his infamous 'text-message womanising'. Also known more for his antics off the field than on is Tasmanian batsman and popular personality David Boon (1960–). 'Boonie' famously drank 52 beers on a plane trip from Australia to England and ate four 72-oz steaks in one hour.

Next up, tennis and Rod Laver (1938–). He was the world's number-one player in 1961, 1962, 1968 and 1969 and is one of only five players to have won all four Grand Slam singles championships – the Australian, French, US and Wimbledon – in a single year. Laver is also the only person to have done it twice, in 1962 and 1969. Evonne Goolagong Cawley (1951–) was the first Australian Aboriginal to win Wimbledon. She also won the Australian Open from 1974 to 1977 and the French Open in 1971. Other Australian tennis greats include Ken Rosewall, John Newcombe and Pat Cash.

In rugby, David Campese (1962–) was the first Australian to play 100 Test matches and is one of the world's most capped players. He was renowned for his speed and trademark 'Goosestep', holding the world record of 64 international tries. In more recent times, scrumhalf George Gregan overtook 'Campo's' record and is now the most capped Australian player.

In swimming, Shane Gould (1956–) was only 15 years old when she won three gold, one silver and a bronze at the 1972 Munich Olympic Games. She broke 11 World Records and 21 Australian Records and then retired aged 16. More recently, Ian Thorpe (1982–) won five Olympic gold medals (in 2000 and 2004), the most won by any Australian, and in 2001 he became the first person to win six gold medals in one World Championship. In total, he won 11 World Championship golds. Nicknamed the 'Thorpedo', young Ian has size 17 feet. He announced his retirement from competition in 2006.

Other sporting greats that have become household names are Greg Norman (golf), Cathy Freeman (athletics) and by no means (if ever) last, Makybe Diva, a racehorse that won the Melbourne Cup three times in a row from 2003 to 2005.

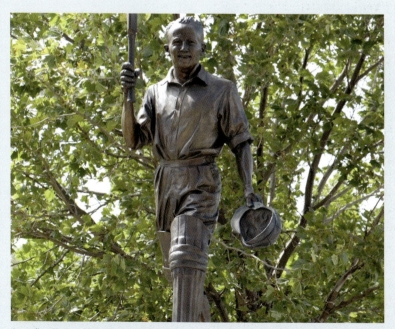

Australian Sir Donald Bradman (1908–2001), nicknamed 'The Don', still rates as the best cricketer of all time

Children

Australia is a wonderful holiday destination for children. Ask any Australian about their own childhood and they will tell you a very large part of growing up 'down under' involves being outside on the beach, in a boat, a 4WD vehicle or a favourite campsite. With careful supervision there is a multitude of excellent, safe venues to keep children happily entertained – with the beach, the cities' modern museums and the theme parks on the Gold Coast of particular note.

Accommodation is generally no problem, with only a few of the upmarket, exclusive retreats focused on romantic getaways unable to accept children. Many motor parks in particular are very well geared up for kids, with adventure playgrounds and child-safe swimming pools.

Many tourist-based activity operations are directed at the children's market and almost every attraction or activity offers family concessions or reduced rates for children.

Some eateries welcome children, while others may decline. In general you are advised to stick to eateries that

Many Australian children practically grow up on the beach

are obviously child-friendly or ask before making a booking.

Beach

Little needs to be said here other than the need to keep a hat on little heads under the sun and apply copious amounts of sun block. Also counsel your charges on the need to swim between the flags and recognise what a lifeguard looks like.

You will generally find most public beaches are patrolled from December to March, with some in the cities having a year-round presence. In Sydney, Bondi, Manly, Balmoral and Coogee are all good, safe options, with many having man-made pools. In Brisbane don't miss the inner-city beach and Lagoon complex (*see p77*) on the South Bank.

Theme parks

The Gold Coast theme parks may be kid heaven, but you will watch your money disappear as fast as ice cream in the midday sun. With the choice of **Sea World**, **Movie World** and **Wet 'n' Wild** (*see pp68–9 & 165*), to name but three, you will not be short of choice and perhaps the best thing to do is to focus on one park, either for a single visit or over a few days with a multi-entry pass.

Wildlife

Despite its misinformed reputation for baby-snatching dingoes, man-eating sharks, poisonous snakes and spiders, wildlife is a fundamental component of

Sun savvy

the Australian holiday experience for both young and old. If you are at all concerned about the rumoured threat of Australia's native wildlife, take a trip to Sydney's **Taronga Zoo** (*see p43*), or indeed any of the numerous wildlife parks up and down the East Coast. Whether captive or not, Australia's abundant wildlife offers one of the greatest natural history education platforms for children on the planet and provided that your child does not launch his ice-cream cone at 'Brutus' the sleeping 320kg (705lb) crocodile, encounters with wildlife can become any foreign child's fondest memory. Australian children have a very healthy respect and love for the outdoors and wildlife borne through exposure and good education. As such, mixing with Australian kids is an ideal way for yours to learn.

Essentials

Arriving
By air

The vast majority of travellers arrive by air into Sydney or Melbourne. The principal international airport for East Coast Australia is Sydney, but Brisbane and Cairns also offer an alternative if you are travelling on an RTW (Round the World) ticket.

There are many international carriers, with **Qantas** (Australia's main airline, *www.qantas.com.au*), **Air New Zealand** (*www.airnewzealand.com*) and **Emirates** (*www.emirates.com*) the main players.

If you are travelling from Europe or North America, an expensive long-haul flight is unavoidable, but from Europe this can be treated as an opportunity for a brief stop-over either in the US (Los Angeles or San Francisco), the Middle East (Dubai), or Asia (Singapore, Bangkok or Kuala Lumpur). Most airlines can help you to offset your carbon footprint.

Fares are high during December and January unless booked well in advance. Mid-year tends to see the cheapest fares. The Internet is the best place to secure cheap flights. If arriving from or via the US you will be granted two pieces of hold luggage up to a total of 75kg (165lb), plus one carry-on item per person, while all other routes only allow one piece per person at 20kg (44lb) plus carry-on.

Sydney's **Kingsford Smith Airport** is 9km (5½ miles) south of the city centre (*www.sydneyairport.com*). The fastest and most convenient way into town is via the Airport Link rail service every 10–15 minutes (A$14). Taxis available outside the terminal take 30 minutes and cost around A$35. Various independent or courtesy shuttles also operate door-to-door.

By sea

Cruise liners regularly visit Australia on World, Pacific or New Zealand and Australia tours. The main ports of call are Sydney and Melbourne and the main players are **Princess Cruises** (*www.princess.com*) and **P&O** (*www.pocruises.com*). Fly-cruise packages are an option.

Customs

The limits for duty-free goods brought into the country include 2.25 litres of alcohol per person (18 years or over) and 250 cigarettes or 250g of cigars or tobacco. There are various import restrictions primarily involving live plants and animals, plant and animal materials (including wood) and foodstuffs. Declare any such items if you are unsure (*see www.customs.gov.au*).

Electricity

The current in Australia is 240/250V AC. Plugs have 2 or 3 blade pins. To use

Street art depiction of the infamous (now deceased) 'Crocodile Hunter', Steve Irwin

appliances from the UK or US you will need an adaptor.

Internet
Fast connection is readily available in Internet outlets, cafés, libraries and most accommodation, though rural areas can be a problem. Wireless capability is improving but is not as widespread as in Europe or the US.

Money
The Australian dollar ($, or A$ to distinguish it from other dollar currencies) is divided into 100 cents (c). Coins come in denominations of 5c, 10c, 20c, 50c, $1 and $2. Banknotes come in denominations of $5, $10, $20, $50 and $100.

Most operators and outlets accept all the major credit cards. You can withdraw cash from ATMs (cashpoints) with a cash card or credit card issued by most international banks, and they can also be used at banks, post offices and bureaux de change.

Traveller's cheques are accepted for exchange in banks, large hotels, post offices and large gift shops. The four major banks – Westpac, Commonwealth, NAB and ANZ – are usually the best places to change money and traveller's cheques, as they offer the best rates and branches are commonplace. Bureaux de change are located at all major airports and in the city centres.

Opening hours
Banks are usually open Mon–Fri 9.30am–4 or 5pm, offices Mon–Fri 8.30am–5pm, and shops Mon–Fri 9am–5.30pm, Sat 9am–5pm and Sun 11am–5pm, although many city outlets remain open later. Many convenience stores and supermarkets are open seven days until mid evening or late at night.

Passports and visas
All travellers to Australia, except New Zealand citizens, must have a valid visa to enter Australia. This must be arranged prior to travel (allow two months) and cannot be organised at Australian airports. Tourist visas are free and are available from your local Australian Embassy or High Commission or, in some countries, in electronic format (an Electronic Travel Authority or ETA) from their websites, and from selected travel agents and airlines. Passport holders from most

European countries, the US and Canada are eligible to apply for an ETA. Tourist visas allow visits of up to three months within the year after the visa is issued. If you are visiting for longer than three months, or are not eligible for an ETA, you may be able to apply for a Visitor or Work Visa. For details visit *www.etaimmi.gov.au*

Pharmacies

Pharmacies are widely available in most centres with at least one open late or 24 hours. Addresses and map locations can be found in the yellow pages (*www.yellowpages.com.au*).

Post

Australia Post has outlets (often called 'Postshops') in all the main centres. Opening hours follow standard business hours with the exception of some major town and city outlets, which may also open on Saturday mornings. Normal post boxes are red while express ones are yellow. For details see *www.auspost.com.au*

Public holidays

1 January – New Year
26 January – Australia Day
March/April (variable) – Good Friday and Easter Monday
25 April (variable) – ANZAC Day
May (variable) – NSW Labor Day (Oct in QLD)
9 June (variable) – Queen's Birthday
25 and 26 December – Christmas and Boxing Day

Smoking

About 17 per cent of Australians are smokers. Smoking is now illegal in pubs, restaurants, cafés and most public buildings (including airports). It is also prohibited on all forms of public transport (including taxis). Many establishments do, however, accommodate smokers in covered, outdoor areas.

Suggested reading and media

The main nationwide daily is *The Australian* (Mon–Fri, with weekend edition). In Sydney and NSW the main newspaper is the *Sydney Morning Herald* (Mon–Fri, with weekend edition). In Brisbane and Queensland it is the *Courier Mail* (Mon–Sat, with Sunday edition). The *Australian Geographic* magazine (*www.australiangeographic.com.au*) is recommended.

Telephoning eastern Australia from abroad
Dial the international prefix followed by 61, then the state phone code minus the first 0, then the 8-digit number.
Note: There are no area phone codes in Australia, just state codes:
ACT/NSW 02
QLD 07
VIC 03
Telephoning abroad from Australia
Dial 0011 followed by the country code:
New Zealand 64
South Africa 27
USA and Canada 1
UK 44
Directory enquiries: 1223
International directory enquiries: 1225

The main TV channels are the highly commercial, mainstream channels 7, 9 and 10, with less sensationalist material offered by ABC and SBS. The subscription Foxtel (Sky) TV is also popular, especially for sports coverage.

Tax

Almost all goods in Australia are subject to a Goods and Services Tax (GST) of 10 per cent. Certain shops can deduct the GST if you show a valid departure ticket. For details see *www.customs.gov.au*

Telephones

Most public payphones are operated by Telstra (*www.telstra.com.au*). Some take phone cards, available from newsagents and post offices, and credit cards. There are many mobile phone companies, including Telstra, Vodafone and Optus. By far the cheapest way of calling overseas is to use an international pre-paid phone card (e.g. Yabba or E-Phone) available from city post offices and newsagents.

Time

Australia covers three time zones, with Queensland and New South Wales using Eastern Standard Time (GMT+10 hours). In NSW, daylight saving means clocks go forward one hour from October to March.

Toilets

Toilets are widely available, free and generally of a good standard. At the beach a toilet and shower block is often attached to the many publicly accessible surf life-saving clubs.

Travellers with disabilities

Facilities for disabled travellers are generally good, especially in the main centres. Many accommodation, transport and activity operators provide facilities, and most major sights and attractions and even parks generally have good access. **Access Foundation** can provide details (*Suite 33, 61 Marlborough St, Surry Hills, NSW. Tel: (02) 9310 5732. www.accessibility.com.au*). In Sydney the free leaflet *CBD Access Map Sydney* is available from visitor information centres.

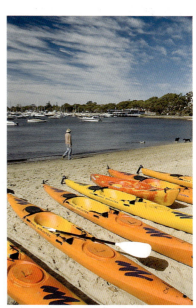

Kayaks tempting exploration of Sydney Harbour

Essentials

Language

English is the main language, but many words and sayings are specific to the country. Australian English is sometimes referred to as 'Strine'. Of course some words like 'mate' are known the world over, but you must beware of stereotypes.

Common words and phrases

arvo	afternoon
bananabender	someone from Queensland
beauty ('bewdy')	excellent, fantastic (often preceded by 'you')
billy	kettle (non-electric)
bludger	layabout, lazy person
bottleshop ('bottle-o')	off-licence or liquor outlet
chook	chicken
chunder	vomit
dag or daggy	dirty wool around sheep's backend, also 'uncool'
doona	duvet
dunny	toilet
esky	portable cool box
fair dinkum	fair, the truth
grommet	young surfer
hard yakka	hard work
jug	kettle (electric)
larrikin	mischievous person
lay-by	keep aside until paid for
mullet	hairstyle (especially 1980s)
no worries	not a problem, no bother
op-shop	second-hand shop
park	parking space
pokies	gambling slot machines
rego	car registration
ripper	excellent (often preceded by 'you')
score	to secure something (often for free), or a date with a girl
She'll be right	Everything will be OK
slab	crate of beer, usually 24 bottles or cans
smoko	work break
snag	sausage
stubbie	can of beer
swag	canvas sleeping bag and mattress in one
thongs	flip-flops
tinnie	can of beer or a small aluminium boat
tucker	food
ute	utility vehicle
yabby	edible freshwater crustacean similar to lobster

Emergencies

Emergency numbers

Police, fire brigade and ambulance 000

Health care

Australia has a national, government-funded health-care scheme called Medicare together with a private health-care network. Public hospitals are part of Medicare and most doctors are registered so that their services can be funded or subsidised by the scheme. Australia has reciprocal arrangements with a handful of countries, which allows citizens of those countries to receive free 'immediately necessary medical treatment' under the Medicare scheme, but this does not include travel by ambulance. Check with your travel agent or national health scheme to check whether you qualify for Medicare and what documents you will require in Australia to claim. All visitors are, however, strongly advised to take out medical insurance for the duration of their visit.

No vaccinations are required for entry into Australia but you are advised to get a tetanus booster. The **Travellers Medical and Vaccination Centre** (TMVC) operates several clinics around the country, including in Sydney (*Level 7, 428 George St. Tel: (02) 9221 7133. www.tmvc.com.au*). Medical facilities in individual towns and cities are listed in the telephone directories. See also *www.health.gov.au*

Health risks

When it comes to personal safety, Australia certainly has its dangers, but with a little common sense and basic precautions they are relatively easy to minimise. The sun is a major factor. UV levels can soar in Australia, with safe exposure limits as low as three minutes, so wear a hat and sunglasses and use sun block. Also be careful of dehydration and drink plenty of fluids.

With long-distance road travel usually a necessity, beware of fatigue as well as large native or stock animals (especially kangaroos and wombats in rural areas at dawn or dusk). Hitchhiking is not recommended.

Palm trees offer some shade from the sun's heat at Dunk Island Resort

Currents can be dangerous, so never swim alone

On the beach always swim between the patrolled flags and be aware of hidden dangers like rips (strong offshore undertows). Avoid swimming alone, and keep swimming partners in sight. While snorkelling or diving, do not touch any creatures or coral. In summer, members of Surf Life Saving Australia patrol many public beaches and they are always the best source for advice and assistance (*www.slsa.asn.au*).

Australia has a terrible reputation when it comes to sharks and poisonous wildlife but, though there are some very real dangers, the threats are over-exaggerated and with a little common sense your encounters with wildlife will be nothing but pleasant. Shark attacks do occur but are extremely rare. Snakes and spiders will generally get out of your way unless harassed, and by avoiding swimming in the ocean north of Townsville from November to March you will avoid the well-publicised risk of marine stingers (potentially fatal small jellyfish) or other venomous sea creatures.

Crime
Australia has average crime rates and tourists are often targeted in both urban and rural areas. The common-sense approach therefore applies to personal safety and possessions. Travel insurance is recommended with premium add-ons that include specific expensive items like cameras or laptops. Check the small print!

Embassies and consulates
Canada
Level 5, 111 Harrington St, Sydney.
Tel: (02) 9364 3000.
Germany
13 Trelawney St, Woollahra, Sydney.
Tel: (02) 9328 7733.
New Zealand
Level 10, 55 Hunter St, Sydney.
Tel: (02) 9223 0222.
South Africa
Level 38, Central Plaza I, corner of Queen St & Creek St, Brisbane.
Tel: (07) 3258 6691.
UK
Level 16, The Gateway, 1 Macquarie Pl, Sydney. Tel: (02) 9251 6201.
USA
19–29 Martin Pl, Sydney.
Tel: (02) 9373 9200.

Directory

Accommodation price guide

Prices of accommodation are based on a double room (or a powered site at a motor park) per night for two people sharing in the high season (with breakfast where applicable).

★	up to A$50
★★	A$51–A$150
★★★	A$151–A$250
★★★★	over A$250

Eating out price guide

Prices are based on an average three-course meal for one, without drinks.

★	up to A$15
★★	A$16–A$25
★★★	A$26–A$30
★★★★	over A$30

SYDNEY

ACCOMMODATION

Australian Heritage Hotel ★★
Along with the Lord Nelson (*see below*) this is a Sydney classic with a mixed clientele and good atmosphere right in the heart of The Rocks.
100 Cumberland St, The Rocks.
Tel: (02) 9247 2229. www. australianheritagehotel.com.
Open: daily 11am–late.

Lord Nelson Pub and Hotel ★★
Fine historic hotel in the edge of The Rocks, which has some very pleasant and affordable en suites above the pub. The added attraction here is the home-brewed beer and general ambience. The pub loses fairly early at night, so noise is generally not a problem.
Corner of Kent St & Argyle St, The Rocks.
Tel: (02) 9251 4044.
www.lordnelson.com.au

Glenferrie Lodge ★★–★★★
Large 3-star, 70-room Victorian mansion in a quiet location yet only a short walk from Kirribilli, ferry terminals and the Harbour Bridge. Full range of shared, single, twin or doubles, some with a balcony and city view. Cheap quality dinners and breakfast buffets.
12A Carabella St.
Tel: (02) 9955 1685. www. glenferrielodge.com.au

Trickett's Luxury B&B ★★★
A restored Victorian mansion in Glebe, 'the village within the city'. Spacious, nicely appointed en suites with antiques and Persian rugs throughout. Off-street parking and generous continental breakfast.
270 Glebe Point Rd.
Tel: (02) 9552 1141.
www.tricketts.com.au

Park Hyatt ★★★★
Hugely popular thanks to its waterside location overlooking the Sydney Opera House. Faultless in presentation, with all

mod-cons and a fine restaurant on the ground floor proving the ideal spot to watch the activity on the harbour.
*7 Hickson Rd.
Tel: (02) 9241 1234. www.sydney.park.hyatt.com*

EATING OUT
Harry's Café de Wheels ★
Dispensing famously yummy pies with pea toppings and gravy at all hours of the night and day, Harry's is something of a Sydney institution. One is surely never enough.
*Corner of Cowper Wharf Rd & Brougham St, Woolloomooloo.
Tel: (02) 9357 3074.
Open: daily 24 hours.*

Botanic Gardens Restaurant ★–★★
A fine escape from the city, with the added attraction of a nearby colony of flying foxes (fruit bats). Utterly clean, enchanting and mesmerising – and that's just the bats.
*Mrs Macquarie's Rd, City.
Tel: (02) 9241 2419.
Open: Mon–Fri noon–3pm, Sat & Sun 9.30am–3pm.*

Doyle's on the Beach ★★★–★★★★
Arguably Sydney's best-known seafood beachside in the eastern suburb of Watsons Bay. The general atmosphere and views across the harbour and city skyline are hard to beat. If you can, book a balcony seat. Sunday afternoons are especially popular and you can combine the trip with a walk around the heads. Book ahead.
*11 Marine Parade.
Tel: (02) 9337 2007.
www.doyles.com.au.
Open: daily noon–3pm & 6–9pm.*

Forty-one Restaurant ★★★★
Even without the commanding views across the Botanic Gardens and harbour, this long-established favourite is deserving of an international reputation for fine dining. Intimate yet relaxed. Bookings essential.
*Chifley Tower, 2 Chifley Square, City.
Tel: (02) 9221 2500.
www.forty-one.com.au.
Open: lunch Tue–Fri from noon; dinner Mon–Sat from 6pm.*

ENTERTAINMENT
Bangarra
An excellent contemporary Aboriginal dance group.
*Wharf 4, Walsh Bay.
Tel: (02) 9251 5333.
www.bangarra.com.au*

Hayden Orpheum Cinema
Fully restored art deco cinema offering a fine alternative to the more modern city cinemas.
*180 Military Rd, Cremorne.
Tel: (02) 9908 4344.
www.orpheum.com.au*

Home Nightclub
Dubbed a 'super club' and spread over four levels, this is one of the country's largest. Here, you can even 'kinkidisco' – the mind boggles.
*Cockle Bay Wharf, Darling Harbour.
Tel: (02) 9266 0600.
www.homesydney.com.
Open: 10pm–6am.
Admission charge.*

Lord Dudley
Takes some finding but this intimate English-style pub deep in the Paddington suburbs is

well worth the effort. Also offers some good pub grub.
236 Jersey Rd.
Tel: (02) 9327 5399.
www.lorddudley.com.au.
Open: Mon–Wed 11am–11pm, Thur–Sat 11am–midnight, Sun noon–10pm.

Opera House and Concourse

The Opera House hosts five performance venues offering everything from Billy Connolly to Andrea Bocelli. Prices and seats range from about A$35 to A$200.

There are also several bars with open-air tables in the shadow of the great Opera House and overlooking Circular Quay and the Harbour Bridge. For casual drinks there is arguably no place more quintessentially Sydney than this, but beware: the drinks are heavily over-priced and it does get very busy.
Box office.
Tel: (02) 9250 7777.
www.soh.nsw.gov.au

Wharf Theatre

Home of the world-renowned Sydney Theatre Company.
Pier 4, Hickson Rd, The Rocks.
Tel: (02) 9250 1999.
www.sydneytheatre.org.au

SPORT AND LEISURE
Bonza Bike Tours

Attack the sights with pedal power, guided or self-guided options from two hours to half a day. Independent hire is also available.
30 Harrington St, The Rocks.
Tel: (02) 9247 8800.
www.bonzabiketours.com

Bridge Climb

The famous ascent of the 134m (440ft) Harbour Bridge span. The three-hour climb can be done day or night in most weather conditions. Stunning views.
5 Cumberland St, The Rocks.
Tel: (02) 8274 7777.
www.bridgeclimb.com

Manly Surf School

Good-value daily classes from 11am to 1pm.
North Steyne Surf Club, Manly Beach.
Tel: (02) 9977 6977.
www.manlysurfschool.com

Sydney by Sail

Based at the National Maritime Museum and offering day trips and introductory lessons.
Festival Pontoon.
Tel: (02) 9280 1110.
www.sydneybysail.com

Sydney Harbour Kayaks

Explore the inner harbour inlets and bays. Guided or self-guided trips.
Spit Bridge, Mosman.
Tel: (02) 9960 4389. www. sydneyharbourkayaks.com. au

NSW NORTH COAST
Byron Bay
ACCOMMODATION
Rae's on Watego ★★★★

Regularly voted one of the top small hotels of the world. Overlooking Watego's Beach near Byron Bay it has all one might expect, including a quality restaurant (open to non-guests).
Byron Bay.
Tel: (02) 6685 5366.
www.raes.com.au.
Restaurant open: lunch, daily noon–3pm; dinner, daily 6.30–10pm.

EATING OUT
Thai Lucy ★★

Good variety, value and lots of atmosphere. Book ahead.

Bay Lane, Byron Bay.
Tel: (02) 6680 8083.
Open: Tue–Sun for lunch
and dinner.

Vegasm ★★

The name speaks for
itself! Also welcomes
non-vegans. Excellent
home-made cream
cheese a speciality.
130 Johnson St, Byron
Bay. Tel: (02) 6680 7080.
Open Mon–Sat 5–9pm.

ENTERTAINMENT

Byron Beach Hotel

Set right beside the beach
and in the heart of Byron
Bay, this is the social
focus of the town both
day and night, with a
lively atmosphere often
spilling out onto a beer
garden. Live bands
Thur–Sun.
Bay St, Byron Bay.
Tel: (02) 6685 6402.
www.beachhotel.com.au.
Open: daily for breakfast,
lunch & dinner.

Pighouse Flicks Cinema

Based alongside the Arts
Factory and housed in
the old piggery, this is
something of a Byron
institution with its quirky
décor and in-house pizza
restaurant. Cult and art-
house movies nightly.

Gordon St via Butler St,
Byron Bay.
Tel: (02) 6685 5828

SPORT AND LEISURE

**Buddha Gardens
Balinese Day Spa**

Health and beauty
treatments.
21 Gordon St, Byron Bay.
Tel: (02) 6680 7844.
Open: daily 10am–6pm.

**Byron Bay Kite-
boarding**

Take an introductory
lesson or a full-day class.
Byron Bay.
Tel: 0402 008 926. www.
byronbaykiteboarding.com

**Byron Bay Skydiving
Centre**

Stunning views and
tandem jumps at up to
3,500m (12,000ft).
Courses available.
Tyagarah Airfield, Byron
Bay. Tel: 1800 800 840.
www.skydivebyronbay.com

Byron Bay Surf School

Various options from
single lessons to multi-
day courses.
127 Jonson St.
Tel: 1800 707 274. www.
byronbaysurfschool.com

Dolphin Sea Kayaking

Half-day tours around
the headlands, often
with dolphin encounters.

9 Marvell St, Byron Bay.
Tel: (02) 6685 8044.
www.dolphinkayaking.
com.au

Coffs Harbour

ACCOMMODATION

**Friday Creek
Retreat ★★★–★★★★**

Luxury, self-contained
cottages with spa and
open fires in a quiet
country setting 17km
(10¹/₂ miles) inland
from Coffs Harbour.
Great views, free bike
hire, complimentary
breakfast and dinner
by arrangement.
267 Friday Creek Rd,
Upper Orara.
Tel: (02) 6653 8221.
www.fridaycreek.com

EATING OUT

**Tide and Pilot
Brasserie ★★★**

Award-winning
restaurant offering fresh
seafood in its beach-
themed interior and
outdoor tables alongside
the marina. Follow your
meal with a stroll across
to Muttonbird Island.
Marina Dr, Coffs Harbour.
Tel: (02) 6651 6888.
Open: daily for lunch,
Mon–Sat for dinner.

SPORT AND LEISURE
Jetty Dive
For cruising, diving, fishing, whale- and dolphin-watching. Diving in the Solitary Islands Marine Reserve is a specialty. Whale-watching from June to end of November.
398 High St, Coffs Harbour. Tel: (02) 6651 1611. www.jettydive.com.au
Valery Trails
Horse-trekking with an award-winning breakfast, BBQ, moonlight trips and camp ride-outs, suited to both advanced riders and beginners.
13km (8 miles) south of Coffs. Tel: (02) 6653 4301. www.valerytrails.com.au

Hunter Valley
ACCOMMODATION
Peppers Convent ★★★★
Once home to the Brigidine order of nuns, this former convent is now one of the highest-profile luxury establishments in the Hunter Valley and without doubt a fine place to indulge.
Halls Rd, Pokolbin, Hunter Valley. Tel: (02) 4993 8999. www.peppers.com.au

EATING OUT
Chez Pok
Restaurant ★★★–★★★★
Attached to the luxury Peppers Guest House, this is considered one of the Hunter Valley's best options for fine dining.
Ekerts Rd, Pokolbin. Hunter Valley. Tel: (02) 4993 8999. www.peppers.com.au. Open: breakfast 7–10am, lunch noon–2pm, dinner 7–9pm.

SPORT AND LEISURE
Balloon Aloft
A fine introduction to the Hunter Valley at dawn.
Rothbury, Hunter Valley. Tel: (02) 4938 1955 & 1800 028 568. www.balloonaloft.com

Iluka
ACCOMMODATION
Woody Head Campsite ★
Superb coastal National Parks and Wildlife Service campsite just beside the Bundjalung National Park. Non-powered sites, fires permitted, plus some cabins with cooking facilities. Book well ahead.
Off Iluka Rd, 14km (8 miles) west of the Pacific Highway, 4km (2½ miles) north of Iluka. Tel: (02) 6646 6134. www.nationalparks.nsw.gov.au

Nelson Bay
SPORT AND LEISURE
Quad Bike King
Thrilling quad-bike (ATV) tours of 1–3 hours across the vast Stockton Beach dunes near Newcastle. A great all-weather activity.
Shearwater Drive, Taylors Beach, Nelson Bay. Tel: (02) 4919 0088. www.quadbikeking.com.au

Port Macquarie
ACCOMMODATION
Glasshouse HW Boutique Motel ★★–★★★
Quality modern motel close to the town centre and only a short stroll from the beach.
1 Stewart St, Port Macquarie. Tel: (02) 6583 1200. www.hwmotorinn.com.au

South West Rocks
ACCOMMODATION
Smoky Cape Lighthouse B&B ★★★
Refurbished former keepers' quarters with both self-contained or B&B options, four-poster

bed and stunning views. Book well in advance. *South West Rocks. Tel: (02) 6566 6301. www. smokycapelighthouse.com. au*

EATING OUT
Trial Bay Kiosk ★–★★
Popular café overlooking the Trial Bay Gaol and beach. Good breakfasts. *Trial Bay Gaol, Arakoon, South West Rocks. Tel: (02) 6566 7100. Open: daily 8am–4pm.*

GOLD COAST
ACCOMMODATION
Trekkers ★★
Budget backpacker-style accommodation in a traditional suburban Queenslander. Well-appointed ensuite rooms with TV. Facilities include a pool and garden. Excellent hosts. *22 White St, Surfers Paradise. Tel: (07) 5591 5616. www. trekkersbackpackers.com.au*
Gold Coast Accommodation Service ★★–★★★
A good agency for securing deals on the many self-contained apartment options.

Shop 1, 1 Beach Rd, Surfers Paradise. Tel: (07) 5592 0067. www. goldcoastaccommodation service.com.au
Mouses House ★★★–★★★★
A fine eco-resort option near the Springbrook National Park, with unique themed bush chalets (some with spa). *2807 Springbrook Rd, Springbrook. Tel: (07) 5533 5192. www.mouseshouse.com.au*
Palazzo Versace ★★★★
Usually the pick for visiting VIPs and celebrities, the Versace offers all the 5-star luxuries you might expect, including a stunning indoor/outdoor pool. The hotel sits close to Sea World and next to the Marina Mirage shopping and marina complex. *Sea World Dr, Main Beach. Tel: (07) 5509 8000. www. palazzoversace.com.au*

EATING OUT
Charlie's Restaurant ★★
Popular, convenient and good value. *Cavill Ave Mall. Tel: (07) 5538 5285. Open: 24 hours.*

Oskars ★★–★★★
Excellent Italian cuisine, beachside location and with views right up the coast to Surfers. *43 Goodwin Tce, Burleigh Heads. Tel: (07) 5576 3722. www.oskars.com.au. Open: daily for lunch and dinner.*
Absynthe ★★★
Chic new French-Australian restaurant at Q1 tower, with award-winning French chef Meyjitte Boughenout. *Ground Floor Q1, Hamilton Ave. Tel: (07) 5504 6466. www.absynthe.com.au. Open: lunch Fri only, dinner Mon–Sat.*

ENTERTAINMENT
Cavill Ave Mall and **Orchid Ave** are the main focus for clubbing, with most venues staying open until dawn. Dress is smart casual, and there is usually an admission charge.
Conrad Jupiter's Casino
Two floors of gaming glitz. Dress smartly. *Off Hooker Blvd (Gold Coast Highway), Broadbeach. Tel: (07) 5592 8100.*

www.conrad.com.au.
Open: 24 hours.
Shooters
Just one of the
mainstream nightclubs.
The Mark, 15 Orchid Ave,
Surfers Paradise.
Tel: (07) 5592 1144.
www.shooters.net.au.
Open: Mon midnight–
5am, Tue–Sat 8pm–5am,
Sun 8pm–midnight.

SPORT AND LEISURE
Aries Tours
Reputable tour company
offering a wide range of
options. Good option for
a tour of the Lamington
National Park.
16 Barnett Pl, Molendinar.
Tel: (07) 5594 9933.
www.ariestours.com.au
Cheyne Horan
Good option for the
quintessential Gold
Coast activity: surfing.
Surfers Paradise Life
Saving Club, Corner
of Hanlan Stand &
Esplanade.
Tel: 1800 227 872.
www.cheynehoran.com.au
Theme Parks
The big three are all
easily accessible and can
be combined with multi-
day or venue tickets (see
pp68–9 for details):

Movie World (Pacific
Highway, Oxenford.
Tel: (07) 5573 8485.
www.myfun.com.au.
Open: 10am–5.30pm.
Admission charge.)
Sea World (Main Beach.
Tel: (07) 5588 2205.
www.myfun.com.au.
Open: 10am–5pm.
Admission charge.)
**Wet 'n' Wild Water
World** (Pacific Highway,
Oxenford.
Tel: (07) 5573 8485.
www.myfun.com.au.
Open: 10am–5pm.
Admission charge.)

BRISBANE
ACCOMMODATION
Explorers Inn ★★
Convenient for the city
centre and a good-value
option. Tidy (if small)
doubles/twins and some
family rooms and singles.
In-house restaurant/bar.
63 Turbot St.
Tel: (07) 3211 3488.
www.explorers.com.au
**Brisbane Holiday
Village ★★–★★★**
15km (9 miles) south of
the city. Quiet setting yet
close to shops and the
main highway.
10 Holmead Rd (Logan
Rd exit off SE Freeway).

Tel: (07) 3341 6133. www.
brisbaneholiday.com.au
**Brisbane Northside
Caravan Village ★★–★★★**
Located on the northern
approach, 12km (7½
miles) from the CBD,
this is the best motor
park near the city,
offering a wide range of
options, from luxury
cabins, to non-powered
sites, pool, store and
camp kitchen.
763 Zillmere Rd
(off Gympie Rd).
Tel: (07) 3263 4040. www.
caravanvillage.com.au
**Emporium Boutique
Hotel ★★★**
Chic new hotel in the
heart of Fortitude Valley,
offering a range of studio
suites, from standard to
king spa. Outstanding
cocktail bar and a
rooftop pool.
1000 Ann St,
Fortitude Valley.
Tel: (07) 3253 6999 &
1300 883 611. www.
emporiumhotel.com.au
**Stamford Plaza
Hotel ★★★–★★★★**
One of the best luxury
CBD hotels offering the
full range of luxury
rooms with fine river and
botanical garden views.

All the usual amenities, including the lauded Siggi's Restaurant.
Corner of Edward St & Margaret St.
Tel: (07) 3221 1999.
www.stamford.com.au

EATING OUT
The Summit Restaurant ★★
A firm favourite for visitors and natives alike, with the biggest attraction its superb views across the city and Moreton Bay.
Mount Coot-tha.
Tel: (07) 3369 9922.
Open: daily, lunch from 11.30am, dinner from 5pm; Sun, brunch from 8am.
The Three Monkeys ★★
Funky West End café, especially popular for weekend brunches.
28 Mollison St.
Tel: (07) 3844 6045.
Open: daily 9.30am–11pm.
Montrachet ★★–★★★
Lots of French flair and ambience orchestrated by acclaimed chef Thierry Galichet.
224 Given Terrace, Paddington.
Tel: (07) 3367 0030.
www.montrachet.com.au.
Open: Mon–Fri noon– 3pm & 6–10pm.

Siana ★★–★★★
Set overlooking the river, with a quality fusion of Thai, Chinese and Indian cuisine.
Riparian Plaza, 71 Eagle St. Tel: (07) 3221 3887.
www.siana.com.au.
Open: Mon–Fri for lunch and dinner, Sat from 4pm.
E'cco ★★★
Long-established award-winner owned by internationally acclaimed chef Philip Johnson. Pleasant informal atmosphere.
100 Boundary St, City.
Tel: (07) 3831 8344.
www.eccobistro.com.
Open: lunch, Tue–Fri noon–2.30pm; dinner, Tue–Sat 6pm–late.
Closed: Sun & Mon.

ENTERTAINMENT
Belgian Beer Café
Excellent range of beers, good food and the best beer garden in the city.
169 Mary St, City.
Tel: (07) 3221 0199. www. belgianbeercafebrussels. com.au. Open: daily 11.30am–late.
The Bowery
Classy 'Valley' favourite hailed as Brisbane's best cocktail joint.
676 Ann St, Fortitude Valley. Tel: (07) 3252 0202.
www.thebowery.com.au.
Open: Tue–Sun 5pm–3am.
Cinemas
There are several complexes, including **Dendy** (*346 George St. Tel: (07) 3211 3244*); **Hoyt's Cinemas** (*Myer Centre, 91 Queen St & 167 Queen St. Tel: (07) 3027 9999*).
Conrad Treasury Casino
Over 80 gaming tables and 1,300 gaming machines. Dress smartly.
Top of Queen St Mall.
Tel: (07) 3306 8888.
www.conrad.com.au.
Open: 24 hours.
Queensland Performing Arts Complex
Main focus of the city's cultural entertainment. Programme includes Queensland's own ballet, opera, orchestra and theatre companies.
Corner of Grey St & Melbourne St, South Bank. Tel: (07) 3840 7444. www.qpac.com.au

SPORT AND LEISURE
Haunted Brisbane Ghost Tour
Entertaining coach and walking options to the

city's most infamous crime scenes.
Tel: (07) 3344 7265. www.ghost-tours.com.au

Kookaburra River Queen paddle steamers offer lunch and dinner sightseeing options.
Tel: (07) 3221 1300. www.kookaburrariverqueens.com

Mirimar Boat Cruises combine a cruise upriver with a visit to the Lone Pine Koala Sanctuary.
Tel: (07) 3221 0300. www.mirimar.com. Departures from North Quay 10am.

River Cruising
There are several options, from paddle steamers to the hop-on hop-off **City Cat** service (*Riverside City Cat terminal. Tel: (07) 3229 7778. www.brisbaneferries.com.au*).

Riverlife Adventure Centre
Abseiling and rock-climbing, kayaking and bike and rollerblade hire.
Naval Stores, Kangaroo Point. Tel: (07) 3891 5766. www.riverlife.com.au

Story Bridge Adventure Climb
Offers a two-hour adventure to a height of 80m (262ft) with views across the city. Dawn or dusk recommended.
170 Main St. Tel: (07) 3514 6900. www.storybridgeadventureclimb.com.au

SUNSHINE COAST AND FRASER COAST
Fraser Island
ACCOMMODATION
Kingfisher Bay Resort ★★−★★★★
Multi-award-winning resort and one of the best in Australia. Classy, harmonious architecture, superb facilities and a variety of accommodation options, from self-contained holiday villas to lodges and luxury hotel rooms. The resort also offers a wide range of in-house activities and tours, or you can hire your own 4WD vehicle.
Kingfisher Bay, Fraser Island. Tel: (07) 4125 5511 & 1800 072 555. www.kingfisherbay.com

SPORT AND LEISURE
Air Fraser Island
Excellent flight and 4WD hire combos to Fraser Island (with camping gear) from around $250 per day.
Fraser Island. Tel: (07) 4125 3600. www.airfraserisland.com.au

Fraser Explorer Tours
Day tours from Hervey Bay.
PMB 1, Urangan. Tel: (07) 4194 9222. www.fraserexplorertours.com.au

Fraser Island Company
Offers a good range of day or multi-day safaris.
Urangan Boat Harbour, Hervey Bay. Tel: 1800 063 933 & (07) 4125 3933. www.fraserislandco.com.au

Hervey Bay
ACCOMMODATION
Colonial Backpackers Resort YHA ★★−★★★
Excellent budget option offering luxury villas, cabins and ensuite doubles. Good bistro/bar, pool, spa and tours desk.
Corner of Pulgul St & Boat Harbour Dr, Hervey Bay. Tel: (07) 4125 1844. www.yha.com.au

EATING OUT
Salt Café ★★
Part of the Peppers complex and considered one of the best venues for fine dining in the area.

Shop 5, 569 Esplanade
Peppers Pier Resort,
Urangan, Hervey Bay.
Tel: (07) 4124 9722.
www.saltcafe.com.au.
Open: daily 7am–5pm.

Sport and leisure
**Mikat Whale Watch
Safari**
Cruises on large
catamarans from
Urangan, Hervey Bay.
Tel: (07) 4125 2343.
Tasman Venture II
Catamaran cruises
exploring the inaccessible
beaches of Fraser Island's
west coast, with
snorkelling and perhaps a
bit of dolphin watching.
Hervey Bay.
Tel: 1800 620 322. www.
tasmanventure.com.au
Whalesong
Also offers cruises on
large catamarans from
Urangan, Hervey Bay,
plus year-round, half-day
dolphin cruises.
Tel: (07) 4125 6233.
www.whalesong.com.au

Noosa
Accommodation
**Noosa River Caravan
Park ★–★★★**
The best motor
park/camping option in
Noosa. Riverside
location. Book at least
two days in advance.
Russell St, Noosaville.
Tel: (07) 5449 7050.

Eating out
Aromas Café ★–★★★
Spacious and modern
with a Mediterranean-
influenced menu. They
also serve excellent coffee
and the streetside
location is a great spot to
watch the world go by.
32 Hastings St, Noosa
Heads. Tel: (07) 5474 9788.
Open: 7am–late, Fri &
Sat 7am–1am.
Bistro C ★★★
Modern Australian cuisine
with good seafood,
overlooking the beach.
On the Beachfront
Complex, 49 Hastings St,
Noosa Heads.
Tel: (07) 5447 2855.
www.bistroc.com.au.
Open: daily for breakfast,
lunch & dinner.

Sport and leisure
Beyond Noosa
Scenic lunch river cruises
to Lake Cootharaba, with
an optional 4WD combo
that takes in the main
sights of the Great Sandy
National Park.
Noosa. Tel: (07) 5449 9177.
www.beyondnoosa.com.au
Camel Company
One- to two-hour
adventure camel safaris
along Forty Mile Beach.
Weight restriction of
95kg (210lb).
North Shore, Noosa.
Tel: (07) 5442 4402. www.
camelcompany.com.au
Kayak Noosa
Sea kayaking around the
Noosa National Park.
Excellent river trips, too.
Independent hire is also
available.
Noosa.
Tel: (07) 0448 567321.
www.kayaknoosa.com
Noosa Hinterland Tours
Take in wineries and the
Glass House Mountains,
Eumundi Markets
(Wed & Sat), and even
Australia Zoo, on request.
Noosa.
Tel: (07) 5446 3111.
www.noosahinterlandtours.
com.au

CAPRICORN AND
CENTRAL COAST
Airlie Beach
Accommodation
**Island Getaway Caravan
Resort ★–★★★**
Four-star motor park
with full facilities.

Corner of Shute Harbour
Rd & Jubilee Pocket Rd,
Airlie Beach.
Tel: (07) 4946 6228.

**Airlie Waterfront
B&B ★★★**
One of the best B&Bs in
the region. Stay-and-sail
packages available.
Corner of Broadwater St
& Mazlin St, Airlie Beach.
Tel: (07) 4946 7631. www.
airliewaterfrontbnb.com.au

EATING OUT
**Deja vu at the
Courtyard ★★**
Intimate, French-
influenced restaurant.
Shop 5, 301 Shute
Harbour Rd, Airlie Beach.
Tel: (07) 4946 5700.
Open: Tue–Sat 6–10pm.

SPORT AND LEISURE
**Fantasea (Blue Ferries)
Cruises**
Whitsunday Island
cruising. The major player
with fast catamarans.
Tel: (07) 4946 5111.
www.fantasea.com.au

Ocean Rafting
Faster option to
Whitehaven Beach on
board a rigid inflatable.
Includes snorkelling and
guided rainforest and
Aboriginal cave walk.

Tel: (07) 4946 6848.
www.oceanrafting.com.au

Whitehaven Xpress
Offers good day trips to
Whitehaven.
Tel: (07) 4946 1585. www.
whitehavenxpress.com.au

Bundaberg
ACCOMMODATION
**Turtle Sands Tourist
Park ★–★★**
3-star motor park within
walking distance of the
Mon Repos turtle
rookery information
centre.
Mon Repos Beach, near
Bundaberg.
Tel: (07) 4159 2340.
www.turtlesands.com.au

Hinchinbrook Island
SPORT AND LEISURE
**Hinchinbrook Ferries
Eco-Tours**
Full-day Hinchinbrook
Island discovery trips.
Cardwell.
Tel: (07) 4066 8585. www.
hinchinbrookferries.com.au

Mackay
ACCOMMODATION
**Cape Hillsborough
Nature Resort ★★**
Beachfront cabins,
motel units or powered
and non-powered

sites. Small store,
pool, restaurant
and bar.
Casuarina Bay,
Cape Hillsborough
National Park.
Tel: (07) 4959 0152. www.
capehillsboroughresort.
com.au

SPORT AND LEISURE
**Mackay Reeforest
Tours**
Day tours to
Hillsborough and
Eungella national
parks.
Tel: (07) 4959 8360.
www.reeforest.com

Magnetic Island
SPORT AND LEISURE
Red Baron Sea Planes
Unique scenic flights in a
Grumman Sea Cat, the
only one of its type in
the world.
Horseshoe Bay, Magnetic
Island.
Tel: (07) 4758 1556. www.
redbaronseaplanes.com

**Tropicana Guided
Adventure Company**
Multifarious award-
winning 4WD trips on
Magnetic Island.
Harbour Terminal,
Magnetic Island.
Tel: (07) 4758 1800.

Mission Beach and Dunk Island

ACCOMMODATION

Dunk Island Resort

★★–★★★

Island resort in a National Park with beachside units and suites, excellent amenities and a wealth of activities on offer.
Brammo Bay, Dunk Island. Tel: 1300 134 044 & (07) 4068 8199. www.poresorts.com.au

Sejala ★★★

Stunning luxury beachfront villa with private pool or a choice of three arty, self-contained beachside huts.
1 Pacific St, Mission Beach. Tel: (07) 4088 6699. www.sejala.com.au

EATING OUT

Scotty's Beachhouse Bar and Grill ★–★★

Good budget bistro meals and a lively atmosphere.
167 Reid Rd, off Cassowary Drive, Wongaling, Mission Beach. Tel: (07) 4068 8870. Open: daily from 5pm.

SPORT AND LEISURE

Coral Sea Kayaking

Full-day sea kayaking trips to Dunk Island with plenty of time to explore.
Mission Beach. Tel: (07) 4068 9154. www.coralseakayaking.com

Jump The Beach

Tandem skydiving onto Mission Beach or Dunk Island, 2,750–4,250m (9,000–14,000ft).
Mission Beach. Tel: 1800 444 568 & (07) 4031 5466. www.jumpthebeach.com

Rockhampton

ACCOMMODATION

Capricorn Caves Ecolodge and Caravan Park ★–★★★

Handy for visiting the caves.
Capricorn Caves, 23km (14 miles) north of Rockhampton. Tel: (07) 4934 2883. www.capricorncaves.com.au

Coffee House Luxury Apartment Motel ★★

Fine mid-range option close to amenities. Self-contained apartments, executive and standard rooms. Café on site and Internet.
Corner of Williams St & Bolsover St, Rockhampton. Tel: (07) 4927 5722. www.coffeehouse.com.au

Outback station stays ★★
Kroombit Lochenbar Station (*195km/120 miles from Rockhampton. Tel: (07) 4992 2186. www.kroombit.com.au*)
and **Myella Farmstay** (*125km/78 miles southwest of the city. Tel: (07) 4998 1290. www.myella.com*) both offer quality outback stays with activities and tours.

EATING OUT

Criterion ★★–★★★

One of the best traditional hotels, serving local steak.
Quay St, Rockhampton. Tel: (07) 4922 1225. www.thecriterion.com.au. Open: daily for lunch & dinner.

Town of 1770

ACCOMMODATION

Beachshacks ★★–★★★

Self-contained character bungalows complete with thatched roofs overlooking the beach.

578 Captain Cook Dr, Town of 1770.
Tel: (07) 4974 9463.
www.1770beachshacks.com

SPORT AND LEISURE
1770 Environmental Tours and Cruises
Eco-tour/cruise on board an amphibious vehicle (LARC) within the Eurimbula National Park, and day-cruises to Lady Musgrave Island.
Town of 1770 Marina.
Tel: (07) 4974 9422.
www.1770larctours.com.au

Lady Musgrave Cruises
Barrier Reef cruises depart from Town of 1770 (transfers from Bundaberg) for day trips and introductory dives. Whale-watching trips operate between August and October. Camping transfers available.
Tel: 1800 072 110.
www.lmcruises.com.au

Townsville
ACCOMMODATION
Yongala Lodge ★★
Named after the famous local shipwreck. Motel units and Greek/international restaurant, all a short stroll from the waterfront.

Fryer St (off the Strand).
Tel: (07) 4772 4633. www.historicyongala.com.au

EATING OUT
Heritage Café and Bar ★–★★
Relaxed café with a good-value blackboard menu.
137 Flinders St East.
Tel: (07) 4771 2799.
Open: lunch Fri, dinner Tue–Sat.

Bistro One ★★
Well-established and locally popular, especially for seafood.
30–34 Palmer St.
Tel: (07) 4771 6333.
Open: daily 6am–late.

SPORT AND LEISURE
Pleasure Divers
Day or multi-day trips and courses (including *Yongala* wreck).
10 Marine Parade.
Tel: (07) 4778 5788.
www.pleasuredivers.com.au

Yeppoon
ACCOMMODATION
Capricorn Palms Holiday Village ★–★★★
This is the best motor park in the area, with everything from deluxe villas to non-powered sites, a good camp

kitchen and pool.
Wildin Way, Mulambin Beach (just south of Rosslyn Bay).
Tel: (07) 4933 6144. www.capricornpalms.com.au

Ferns Hideaway Resort ★–★★★
Isolated rainforest resort. Colonial-style lodge, log cabins with open fires and spa, budget rooms, campsites and a bar and restaurant.
Byfield, 50km (31 miles) north of Yeppoon.
Tel: (07) 4935 1235.
www.fernshideaway.com.au

CAIRNS AND THE FAR NORTH
Atherton Tablelands
ACCOMMODATION
Pteropus House B&B ★★
Not only a quality B&B with two tidy, self-contained apartments, but also a (separate) working fruit bat hospital.
Corner of Carrington Rd & Hutton Rd, Atherton.
Tel: (07) 4091 2683.
www.athertontablelands.com/bats

Allumbah Pocket Cottages ★★–★★★
Excellent, fully self-contained cottages

complete with spa, ideal for couples. Welcoming owners make sure you get the most out of the region.

24–26 Gillies Highway, Yungaburra.
Tel: (07) 4095 3023. www. allumbahpocketcottages. com.au

Cairns

Accommodation

Cairns Coconut Caravan Resort ★–★★★★
Reputed to be one of the best motor parks in the country.
Bruce Highway (about 6km/3¾ miles south of Cairns, corner of Anderson Rd).
Tel: (07) 4054 6644.
www.coconut.com.au.

Bohemia Resort ★★
Modern motel with spacious doubles and a pool. Regular shuttles to town.
231 McLeod St.
Tel: (07) 4041 7290. www. bohemiaresort.com.au

Sofitel Reef Casino Hotel ★★★–★★★★
Centrally located luxury hotel offering full range of rooms and suites with spa baths and private garden balconies. Award-winning Thai restaurant, rooftop swimming pool and casino.
35–41 Wharf St, Cairns.
Tel: (07) 4030 8888.
www.sofitel.com

Eating out

Swiss Cake and Coffee Shop ★–★★
Restraint impossible, coffee top class.
93a Grafton St.
Tel: (07) 4051 6393.
www.swisscakeandcoffee shop.com.au. Open: Mon–Fri 7am–5pm, Sat 7am–2pm.

Gaura Nitai's Vegetarian ★★
Imaginative and good-value vegetarian café.
55 Spence St.
Tel: (07) 4031 2255.
Open: daily from 6pm.

Ochre Restaurant ★★–★★★
Best bet for Modern Australian cuisine, where you can try kangaroo, crocodile as well as local seafood favourites.
43 Shields St.
Tel: (07) 4051 0100. www. redochregrill.com.au.
Open: lunch, Mon–Fri noon–3pm; dinner, daily 6–10pm.

Entertainment

Reef Casino
Two-level casino at the Sofitel Reef Casino Hotel.
35–41 Wharf St, Cairns.
Tel: (07) 4030 8888.
www.reefcasino.com.au.
Open: 24 hours.

Sport and leisure

Big Cat Green Island Reef Cruises (*Tel: (07) 4051 0444. www. bigcat-cruises.com.au*);
Great Adventures (*Tel: (07) 4044 9944. www. greatadventures.com.au*);
Reef Magic (*Tel: (07) 4031 1588. www.reefmagiccruises.com. au*) and **Sunlover Cruises** (*Tel: 1800 810 512. www.sunlover.com. au*) are the main cruise companies in Cairns.
All are based at the new Reef Fleet Terminal, Spence St.

Cairns Dive Centre (*121 Abbott St. Tel: (07) 4051 0294. www.cairnsdive.com.au*),
Down Under Dive (*287 Draper St. Tel: (07) 4052 8300. www. downunderdive.com.au*) and **ProDive** (*Corner of Abbott St & Shields St.*

*Tel: (07) 4031 5255. www.
prodive-cairns.com.au)*
are just some of the
main players for reef
diving. Day or multi-day
trips, introductory
dives or full courses
are available.
Cairns Heli Scenic
(*City Heliport,
Pier Marketplace.
Tel: (07) 4031 5999. www.
cairns-heliscenic.com.au*),
Daintree Air Services
(*2 Mantra Esplanade,
Shield St.
Tel: (07) 4034 9300.
www.daintreeair.com.au*)
and **Reefwatch Air
Tours** (*GAM Hangar,
Cairns International
Airport. Tel: (07) 4035
9808. www.reefwatch.
com*) all provide fixed-
wing or helicopter
flights over the
rainforest, the reef and
surrounding islands,
from ten-minute jaunts
to longer reef or
rainforest scenic tours.

**Cape Tribulation and
Daintree**
ACCOMMODATION
Red Mill House ★★–★★★
Affordable, quality
B&B option in the heart
of the village. Lovely

gardens and plenty of
wildlife.
*Daintree Village.
Tel: (07) 4098 6233.
www.redmillhouse.com.au*
**Daintree Eco Lodge
and Spa ★★★★**
Internationally
renowned, multi-award-
winning lodge offering
15 luxury villas set in the
rainforest. Full spa
facilities, ecological-
based activities and à la
carte restaurant.
*20 Daintree Rd
(3km/2 miles south of
the village).
Tel: (07) 4098 6100.
www.daintree-ecolodge.
com.au*
**Voyages Silky Oaks
Lodge and Healing
Waters Spa ★★★★**
Another international
award-winner. Deluxe
designer 'riverhouses'
with spa, as well as
free-standing en-suite
chalet doubles (some
with spa) and a fine
restaurant. In-house
activity schedule and
pick-ups available.
*7km (4¹/₂ miles) north
of Mossman.
Tel: 1300 134 044 &
(02) 8296 8010.
www.poresorts.com.au*

Port Douglas
ACCOMMODATION
Marae B&B ★★★
Excellent eco-oriented
B&B 15km (9 miles)
north of Port Douglas.
Three very tidy en-suite
rooms.
*Lot 1, Ponzo Rd,
Shannonvale.
Tel: (07) 4098 4900.
www.marae.com.au*
**Sheraton Mirage
Resort ★★★★**
Large luxury resort
located on the shores
of Four Mile Beach.
The facilities are
faultless and the
pool legendary.
*Davidson St.
Tel: (07) 4099 5888.
www.sheraton-mirage.com*

EATING OUT
**Rainforest Habitat
Wildlife Sanctuary ★★★★**
Entertaining breakfast
and lunch experiences in
the midst of the
sanctuary and
surrounded by tame
birds. Bookings essential.
*Corner of Captain
Cook Highway &
Port Douglas Rd.
Tel: (07) 4099 3235. www.
rainforesthabitat.com.au.
Open: daily 8am–5pm.*

Index

Acknowledgements

Thomas Cook Publishing wishes to thank REBECCA ROBINSON for the photographs in this book, to whom the copyright belongs, except for the following images:

DREAMSTIME/Thorsten 20, Ben Jeayes 58, Susinder 59, Baruse008 60, Spacetray 98, pro6x7 102, Emmaloubarber 124
FLICKR/luvjnx 25, phototram 41, dormousie 52, krossbow 53, hydrolix 60, safaris 78, maedl 84, Preview H 85, Will Ellis 87, Kiwi Mikex 91, WordRidden 122
WORLD PICTURES/PHOTOSHOT 90, 110, 125

For CAMBRIDGE PUBLISHING MANAGEMENT LTD:
Project editor: Rosalind Munro
Typesetter: Paul Queripel
Copy editor: Anne McGregor
Proofreader: Jenni Rainford
Indexer: Karolin Thomas

SEND YOUR THOUGHTS TO
BOOKS@THOMASCOOK.COM

We're committed to providing the very best up-to-date information in our travel guides and constantly strive to make them as useful as they can be. You can help us to improve future editions by letting us have your feedback. If you've made a wonderful discovery on your travels that we don't already feature, if you'd like to inform us about recent changes to anything that we do include, or if you simply want to let us know your thoughts about this guidebook and how we can make it even better – we'd love to hear from you.

Send us ideas, discoveries and recommendations today and then look out for your valuable input in the next edition of this title.

Emails to the above address, or letters to Travellers Series Editor, Thomas Cook Publishing, PO Box 227, Unit 9, Coningsby Road, Peterborough PE3 8SB, UK.

Please don't forget to let us know which title your feedback refers to!